"Make Cash in a Property Market Crash"

D1633484

"Make Cash in a Property Market Crash"

Mark Homer & Rob Moore

www.progressiveproperty.co.uk

Order this book online at www.progressiveproperty.co.uk/book-2-buy-now

Or email ask@progressiveproperty.co.uk

Other books by Rob Moore and Mark Homer can be ordered at www.progressiveproperty.co.uk/book-buy-now

Meet Rob & Mark personally at one of their open days

www.progressiveproperty.co.uk/open-day-offer

Cover design by Nick Hillson

Photography by Nick Hillson

Published by Progressive Property Ltd.

Printed in Peterborough, Cambridgeshire, UK

ISBN: 978-0-9559712-0-4

www.progressiveproperty.co.uk

Suites 5 & 6

Queen Street Chambers

Peterborough

PE1 1PA

0845 1309505

ask@progressiveproperty.co.uk

Skype: rob.progressive

For everyone who forgot to listen to everyone else.

If it wasn't for you

Rob would like to thank Mark. Without him I would not have a squillionth of the knowledge I have about Property now. His eye for detail is, well, eye opening [because he can do the stuff I don't like to do]. I am lucky to have such a good friend as a business partner. It's still exciting and we're one of the few left, aren't we Mark?!

Mum for being Mum Dad for being Dad and doing the things that are essential that most people don't notice. I do, so thank You.

Simon, Catherine, Sharon and Gem for reading the book at the 11th hour and spotting all the mistakes. If there are any more in here, it's their fault! Jenni for listening to endless hours of audio of me talking too much to get the book here and Chris at Forward Press for being so very flexible efficient. Lyndon for saving all the hardware in the office from being thrown out of the window from the second floor. Nick for the awesome design work he does and for doing it quicker than last time! Everyone who is here and reading now, you are the 5%. You are the people who'll succeed. Thank you.

Rob Moore

robmoore@progressiveproperty.co.uk

And if it wasn't for you

Mark would like to thank Mum & William. You have been a massive help in my life, in our business and in my investments. I would never have developed the Property buying skills that I have without your help. Thank You.

I would also like to thank some of the people who have helped to teach me how to buy cheap houses [whether they wanted to or not!]. Sometimes your opponents can help to make you very strong; you know who you are. Thanks.

I would also like to thank Simon for taking over my role and doing it so well. You're going to make a lot of money. You are a big part of turning Progressive into what it is today.

Rob is the best business partner I could have, period. Clever, ferociously hard working, very focused, hugely competent and completely trustworthy. I thank you for all the support you have given me and for being my business partner, the future looks like an unbelievable place.

Mark Homer

markhomer@progressiveproperty.co.uk

Contents

Section 1: Introduction: Sheep & Crabs

Section 2: Getting real

Section 3: The current market

Section 4: Psychology

Section 5: Motivated sellers

Section 6: Accidental to professional investor

Section 7: Learn from their mistakes

Section 8: What are you going to do now?

And for you because not many people do.

Section 1: Introduction

Once again, we've broken the rules. So sue us.

We've gone and written a book in 2 voices. We've gone and written a book which talks about making cash, when everyone else is losing it hand over fist left right and centre.

Most people will tell you that you're crazy to even think about buying Property now. Most people will tell you that you can't make money in Property anymore; it's done. It's all over. Go home and watch Big Brother.

You are about to learn why we love that. We know the rules and the statistics. We need them. You know; the voices, the doubters, the 'Devil's Advocates.'

There is a system for success and *now is the best time* to put that system into practice. More millionaires are made in times of 'recession' than at any other time, according to our good friend, business partner and CEO of Investment Mastery, Marcus de Maria. Well guess what: *now is your chance* to make that happen [while everyone else is waiting for the storm to calm and blow away].

What do Microsoft, Hewlett-Packard and Disney have in common? They all started during economic downturns, as did more than half of the 30 companies that comprise the Dow Jones industrial average.

And here is an interesting quote from bankrate.com:

'Entrepreneurial startups by laid-off and downsized employees, managers and executives often help get the economy growing again.'

There are huge benefits from being in a 'crash' or 'recession.' Think about the reduction in petrol queues [when there's not a shortage], the bargain petrol guzzling Cars you can buy [a latest model Range Rover for £13,000, anyone?], more meals with your family, more business start up opportunities, far more things given out for free [2 for one's, loss leaders and incentives], less junk mail from credit card and loan companies and so on.

They aren't going to make you a millionaire, but the shift from 'doom and gloom' thinking to 'opportunistic' mindset definitely can.

It's all about **what you can do right now** and the massive abundance of opportunity out there.

But only if you're quick now.

Lean in a little, you're going to love this.

Special upfront offer**

If you missed, have not read or did not receive our free bonuses worth £247 that came along with buying our books, then please feel free now to log on to this page anytime:

www.progressiveproperty.co.uk/free-offer-now

About Rob & Mark

Our stories are at the back of the book [again]. There you will read what gives us the right to even talk to you. We had feedback from a dear friend who said we should put ourselves at the front so that you get to know us more. Many of you already know us. Hi!

If not, you'll get to know us very well. But if you want to read our full stories then you can go to the back of the book where there are a few pages that tell you more about us. Because this book is for you, we thought that the back is the best place for them. What we do think is relevant to you now, is how we got to where we are and how you can do the same.

A small introduction:

Mark bought his first Property in 2004:

I started buying small houses, because I realised that the smaller properties [under £125,000] in our area were growing quicker when compared to anything over £150,000. I saw it as reduced risk to chop my money into smaller properties rather than buying expensive ones, and knew that most people want to rent cheaper houses rather than 5 Bed Mansions with swimming pools and cinema rooms [which I couldn't afford anyway].

Having spent ages researching [I have a bit of a habit of over-analysing] I found *one street* in Peterborough that I felt was massively undervalued compared to other streets in the same area of the same type.

I must have bought most of this street and was only spending about £3,000 on full redecorations. I was buying the properties at around £75,000. I was getting them cheap anyway because I was negotiating good discounts, and I was **convinced** that they were worth up to £100,000.

I wanted to get all of my money back out of the properties so that I could keep buying more on that street without any extra cash. I put them all on the market at the same time for what I thought they were really worth. I then got a surveyor round to value them and gave him the comparables of my other houses that I had recently put on the market. I had a couple that were not valued as high as I wanted, so once I got a surveyor that valued one of my properties at the price I wanted, I got him to value all of the others. He valued them all at the price I believed they were worth.

As a result I was able to remortgage these properties almost instantly after revaluation and get all of my money back [deposit, all fees and refurb costs] and extra cash on top, because of the discount I had got, and the value I had added by doing some light refurbishment work.

I kept going until I had pushed the value of the whole street so high that I could not get the properties as cheap anymore. But that was fine because I owned a load of them and they were all free!

And sure enough, as I had predicted, the market grew and the properties continued to go up. In 2 years the properties I bought went up almost 50%.

I knew I had a system that I could just replicate all over Peterborough. All I had to do was locate the areas that were undervalued with good rents, and buy as many as I could using the same strategy.

This one strategy, that took me 3 years to refine, has helped me build a substantial portfolio. We are using the same system very successfully to help our investors do the same.

Since then Progressive has grown to be one of the 2 biggest Property portfolio building companies in the UK. We've had articles in major publications such as 'The Independent' and 'The Wall Street Journal.'

I run a select few mentorships which you can read about in the back of the book. By the time you have read this book they may be of serious interest. I don't run many because it is my personal time, but many of the people I have trained have started buying Property right away almost as quickly as we do, and it feels great [although we are creating competition for ourselves!].

As a result I have learned about nearly every city in the UK, and helped people use our 'Portfolio Building Machine' strategy all over the country.

Rob started Property investment in 2005 having thought about it for 4 years [without taking any action].

Within 3 months of learning this strategy I had already remortgaged my house that I had bought 3 years before. My house had gone up from £125,000 to £170,000 in that time. The funny thing is that I had made £45,000 in 3 years doing nothing at all, from that one Property.

I was an 'accidental investor' [read about the 5 stages of investment later] like so many people who own their own house are. I didn't even know that I was literally sitting on a Goldmine, and *that one house* would help me build an asset base with Mark worth many millions.

As an artist, in that same 3 years, I had struggled working 14 hours or more every day just to earn the same amount of money.

I didn't even buy it at discount; I bid vendor in the balls and negotiated it all the way down to the asking price! My Dad helped me raise the deposit. My diligence and market research went as far as: it's next door to Mum and Dad, I want it.

When I remortgaged my repayments went down from £750 per month to £550 per month. *And* I released £26,000 cash. This was because I had not got the best rate at that time, and because I was on a capital repayment mortgage.

With that remortgage I paid off all of my credit cards and loans [which saved me around £1500 per month] and with what was left I bought another 7 properties, with Mark, in the space of 4 months. I built a portfolio that was worth well over £1million [which keeps going up] before that year was even over [2006]. Since that time we have not stopped buying Property together and we never will.

Why would we? You may not either. Stop, that is.

I literally went from being nearly £30,000 in debt to having a portfolio that could fund the rest of my life, all in less than 6 months. I am certainly nothing 'special,' I was no expert at the time, and Mark had most of the knowledge back then. The one thing I am proud of is that I was *decisive*. I found the strategy that worked and I took immediate action. I have never looked back.

Our portfolio has grown significantly since then and we have built Progressive, helping other people do the same. I totally can't distinguish between work and play. I'm sure that makes me completely boring outside of work, but then Sam Walton was renowned for his passion for 'work' and built the Wall Mart empire, the biggest chain of retail stores worldwide. It is also one of the world's largest companies: bigger than Exxon Mobil, GM and GE.

We have bought over 200 properties for ourselves and our investors. I have spoken at over 50 events in front of thousands of people, and have enjoyed meeting and educating people more than I ever thought I could.

We have been in discussions with many TV production companies and have a new concept for a Property TV show that we intend to launch in the near future, as well as recording a pilot with Channel 4 for a Property documentary.

Enough sizzle, where's my steak?

So that is more than enough about the two of us. Hopefully that has helped you feel excited about what you are about to learn now.

What you are about to read, if applied and persevered with, will absolutely guarantee your future financial success, security and happiness.

It is that simple.

Bring it on? You want it? Well here we go…

One more thing: a huge thank you for buying our book, it really means a lot to us.

Sheep & Crabs

People are like Sheep.

Sheep move in flocks, They herd. They go Baa. Baa.

When one Sheep goes one way, all of the other Sheep follow, don't they? When one Sheep decides that it wants to go and graze on a different bit of grass; the grass that looks green and juicy rather than brown and flat, all the other Sheep follow.

When one Sheep decides that it wants to do something slightly different, something out of the ordinary, something that breaks the mould, all the other Sheep follow.

Sheople [Sheep + People] are interesting. We've all been one from time to time. I'm not saying that you're a Sheep now but at some time in our lives we've all been Sheep. We've all followed the crowd and we've all followed what everybody else does.

Why?

Why on earth would we want to follow everyone else when we all know the statistics? We know that only one person in 100 will become a millionaire. According to research made by CapGemini and Merryl Lynch in the world wealth report, there are 2,669,000 millionaires in the U.S, which is 0.9% of the population. In the whole world there are 8,700,000 millionaires, which is about 0.13% of the population.

Yet the Sheep follow the 99 that will never be one. We still can't work out why.

They're scared aren't they? One of the Laws of Influence [discussed later] is social proof. We are all far more likely to do something if other people are doing it or have done it. Just like Sheep. No one wants to be the first to make the mistake. No one wants to be the first to lose money. No one wants to look stupid!

Stupid, isn't it?

It's funny, because in Texas people brag about how much money they've lost; like it's OK, or even cool, to have risked money. The more we fear failure, or looking silly, the less likely we are to ever achieve anything, and the more likely we are to just go...

Baa.

We know it's early in the book, but let's go into a little bit of detail if that's OK with you. In the study of behaviour and intelligence of Sheep, which you can find on Wikipedia, there are some very interesting findings.

Hefted [definition]: 'the instinct of keeping to a certain small local area throughout life.'

'All Sheep have a tendency to congregate close to other members of a flock.'

'For Sheep, the primary defence mechanism is simply to flee from danger when their flight zone is crossed.'

'Sheep become highly stressed when separated from their flock.'

Baa.

'Even if Sheep survive an attack, they may die simply from panic.'

People can also be just like Crabs.

We have a really interesting story to tell you about Crabs. This is 100%, no word of a lie, the honest truth about what happens when Crab fishermen go fishing. And it's very funny.

Crab fishermen have these huge boxes that they put the Crabs in that they've caught through big landing nets they throw in the sea. Some are tiny, some are gigantic, but one thing is the same; they all have big claws. Compared to the size of their body and their brain; their claws are massive.

Now get this: the Crab fishermen don't actually put a lid on the box that they catch the Crabs in. Do you know why this is? Think about it for a minute...

Oh the suspense must be killing you now.

The fishermen know that if any one of the Crabs tries to leave the box, all the other Crabs will grab the Crab that dares to leave the box with their big claws and pull it back in. True. Really, it is.

Whenever any one of the Crabs thinks to itself:

'Wait a minute, I don't want to be stuck in this box cramped up with all these other Crabs, and boiled in a big hot pan by a French Chef who doesn't have the decency to kill me first, or frozen, or my guts eaten out of a shell. I'm going to get out of this box and jump back into the water [because of course it wouldn't be that difficult to do]. But no, all the other Crabs pull it back in the box.

They're not having any of that. No freedom for you Mr Crab, if I'm stuck in here, then so are you. There's nothing you can do about it and you're going to have the same fate as me.

You might know a song about that?

People can be much more like Sheep and like Crabs than they would actually like to admit [or that they are consciously aware of].

Now, we've all been there and that's OK. I've been there [Rob]. I used to work with my family in our pub before I understood the difference between an asset and a liability, and my sister didn't really like it much either, if she's honest.

I love her dearly, but I know she'll never read this. She'll be too busy reading Jordan's biography, and that's OK too.

So she would have her weekly fall out with my Dad, they would shout at each other and throw bar towels and packets of crisps at each other in front of customers, and she would walk out behind her extended two fingers and vow to never come back.

Sometimes she would get to the door, sometimes she would get as far as the phone and other times she would get all the way to the computer to Monster.co.uk, or even all the way into town to a recruitment agency. But every time, without fail, she would end up back in the pub with her tail between her legs, pulling pints and carving meat the next day.

And I didn't help.

Every time she came to me for support I would dismiss her categorically and let her know in no uncertain terms that she was never going to get anywhere. She had no qualifications, her history was to come back and that is exactly what she would do this time around, so why even bother?

I had big claws.

She didn't need that from me. She didn't need that from anyone. That wasn't going to make her situation any better, was it? She needed a gentle size 10 up the backside or some help and support, but it's funny how hard that is to come by.

And your friends and family can be the worst at that, can't they? I've learned my lessons from that.

When it comes to making money, when it comes to **making huge amounts of money**, creating wealth, building huge Property portfolios and making passive income, then our experience in this life is that people have to act in a way that is against the tide; in a way that doesn't follow like the Sheep do. In a way that doesn't pull back like the Crabs do.

To give you an example of this in the stock market there are some very famous investors: George Soros, Warren Buffet, David Dreman, who are known as 'Contrarian' Investors.

Look at the definition of a 'Contrarian' Investor:

'A Contrarian believes that certain crowd behaviour [flock –we put this bit in!] among investors can lead to exploitable mispricings in securities markets. For example, widespread pessimism about a stock can drive a price so low that it overstates the company's risks, and understates its prospects for returning to profitability. Identifying and purchasing such distressed stocks, and selling them after the company recovers, can lead to above-average gains. Conversely, widespread optimism can result in unjustifiably high valuations that will eventually lead to drops, when those high expectations don't pan out.'

Thanks to Wikipedia for that. Isn't that interesting, we'll come back to this later.

These investors make huge amounts of money in downturns because, putting it simply, they buy when everybody else is selling [or when running away in the flock mentality].

'Sheople' view someone who has cash and is 'cleaning up' in a downturn as someone who is taking advantage of people. We know that's not true in reality. Anyone who has an ounce of intelligence would know that when most people have no money the person who is going to make money is the person who has the money.

'The Golden rule is the man with the Gold, rules!'

When everybody else is selling a trade because they believe the market has bottomed out, the person who is going to make money is the person who can buy all those trades at a cheap price and wait for them to go up.

Property is exactly the same because the **concepts are exactly the same**.

Let us remind you of this: there are **more millionaires made in times of recession** than at any other time. When we say any other time we mean a rising [bull] market or a stagnant [flat] market.

The interesting thing about this **fact** is that statistically there has only been a small amount of time throughout history where we have been through a recession:

'There have been 5 years of full-scale recession in the UK economy during the post-war period. The last recession occurred between 1990-92. Since then the economy has enjoyed the longest sustained growth of national output for over 30 years. Real GDP has increased for 9 years in succession - and at the end of 2000, the UK economy has grown in size (in real terms) by over 20% from the low point (trough) of the last recession.'

Thanks to tutor2u.net, the leading global publisher of internet learning resources for business and economics.

So, for example, we've had the crash in Property in the late 80's and 90's. We're also experiencing what some people are already calling a 'crash' now in 2008, but that's only 3 examples in the last 20 years. If you analyse the data of house prices [source: Nationwide house price statistics] you'll also notice something very interesting. Since 1952 Property has gone down in 1953 [by £19], 1954 [by £10], 1990 [by £4,668], 1991 [by £912], 1992 [by £2019] and in 1995 [by £154]. That's 6 years out of 56, around one in every 9.7 years.

Yet in that small percentage of time, one in every 10 years, more millionaires [many through property] are made than at any other time. That's one tenth of the time that makes more millionaires than 9 tenths of the time, according to the data given by Nationwide.

We're not going to talk down this 'potential crash,' that is for our last book and not for this one. If you can get your head around this concept, then statistically this might be the last chance for 10 years that you can really profit big in one year, or one given period of time.

More about this exact point later, but don't you find that interesting?

So why does this happen?

Only 1% of people are going to become millionaires. The fact that more people [than at any other time] become millionaires through a recession is based on *flock sentiment*.

When we endure a recession, the 99% believe that they can't make money; they believe that everyone is losing money and hey presto that becomes their reality; they lose money. They believe that there is no opportunity in the market because of what they read in the papers, what they hear on TV and what's produced by the mass media. It is fed down the media funnel and what is first gossip becomes expectation, and then it becomes reality. It's propaganda. The 'average' person thinks as the 'average' person thinks, and the 'average' person becomes indoctrinated to believe that there are no opportunities in the market and that we're all losing money.

It must feel like a washing machine; a self fulfilling prophecy of doom.

Baa.

Your guarantee

If, after reading this book, you feel that we have talked utter crap, or that there has been no realisable value in what we have written, we will give you your money back, no questions asked.

Just like we did in "The 44 Most Closely Guarded Property Secrets."

Actually we probably will ask why, because your opinion matters to us, but we'll still stand by our guarantee.

We feel that we have seen so much [and the road is never ending] that if you are just starting out, or even if you have been investing for years, you **need** to know this information if you want to make money from Property right now.

If we can help you avoid and [pre-empt] the mistakes most investors make, then this book has been worth the years, the money, the fun, the pain, the continuous editing and the sweat we have put into it.

Rob Moore & Mark Homer

Why would we offer a money back guarantee on a book? Surely that is ridiculous and unnecessary.

That is a risk we are willing to take to prove to you, before you start, that we feel that there is so much truth out there that you're not being told by most people or companies.

When we wrote our first book, we thought that 1% of you who read our books would want your money back. We now know that's not true, because I analysed the data. It's actually 0.017%. We are proud of that, because it smashes the statistics.

Now we know that it won't be you, but it will be someone. They are the ones who are too tight to take the information, and see more benefit in getting the cash back, the ones who know that they can't be bothered to do anything about it and so see value in getting some beer money back, or the ones who think we are talking bollocks. If you do decide to return it please send it back to Progressive Property where we will refund your investment. All of our details are at the front and back of the book.

The fact is that you have put your hand in your pocket [again], even if it is only a small investment, and that says a lot.

Thank You!

We believe you will want to use this book long into the future for reference to build your portfolio. And you should. You might even enjoy it too.

Don't miss this crash. But if you do, save this book until the next one, you will need it, for sure.

Use it as a manual, use it as a guide, use it as a checklist of do's and don'ts, use it to motivate and inspire you to take action. Use it as a warning as to what and who to watch out for. Use it as a kick up the backside [because we all need it, and there's nothing wrong with that].

Just make sure you use it.

And if at the end of the book you still think to yourself:

'I don't have the time'

'I'm not interested in doing it myself'

Then we will offer you a way where you can have it all, without putting any of your own time or effort in. We will offer you an *even easier* way to make money in Property.

It is stage 5: the leveraged Property investor

Does that sound fair enough?

But you must read all the way to the end of the book to qualify for this, and you will be very glad that you did!

What can you expect from this book?

Information that is relevant *right now*.

Next year or the year after that, this book might gather dust until the next Property crash. You can expect to see a different view of the Property market. If you want more doom and gloom and recession propaganda, then this isn't the book for you.

But if you really want to understand opportunity, if you want to know how millionaires are made and how professional Property investors are made, then this is just the right book for you at just the right time.

There are more millionaires made in a recession than at any other time. You know that already and you'll know why we repeat it in just a second. There are also more professional Property investors made in the time of a Property market downturn, because that is where you make your money.

Make hay now. Be decisive. If you get in there in time; well done. If you don't; don't worry. When this time comes around again, you'll be more prepared than anyone else; with a big pile of cash and the Property hunger of a caged animal!

For your enjoyment and maximum benefit

You will find things repeated in this book. Some of it will be conscious to you, some of it will not. This is intentional, because you know the convincer statistics. If you think you've heard something somewhere before, it may have been in this book, it may have been out there, it could have been while you sleep tonight, but it's going in deep and that is right where you want it to be.

This book is designed to layer content gradually in your mind. It is vital that you read the book cover to cover, and then read it again. Most people only retain 5% of the information in a book. That would be enough, but if we can double or triple that, that additional information alone could **make you a lot of money** over the next couple of years.

The book will build up. The majority of the specific tools, techniques and secrets come further into the book. The psychological preparation to receive and understand those tools and techniques will build up through the first half of the book. You may be tempted to take a peek ahead of schedule, we wouldn't advise it, you might miss something that you really didn't want to miss.

90% of success is how you process what is thrown at you and **the meaning that you attach to events that happen**. The same wind blows on us all: some build Castles of strength and others build paper tents that get blown away.

You have built a strong and solid foundation just getting this far.

What you won't get from this book

Bullshit.

We've seen enough of that.

This book is how it actually is, from our experience.

You won't get rich just reading this book and bags of Gold won't fall on your head.

What we are interested in talking about is what actually works in **reality**. What we have learned, applied, and got **real** results from that we have **measured and tested**. What we know to be the truth based on our own personal experience.

But if you apply what you read, keep going, take decisive action, find mentors and **get perfect later**, then your results will become more in line with what you want, rather than what you already have.

Our disclaimer:

We have taken care to make the figures and specifics in this book as accurate and relevant as possible at the time of writing; and of course we hope you understand that these can change dependent on market and economic forces beyond our control.

The content, projections, figures and indications contained in this book are based on opinion and cannot be relied upon when making investment decisions. As with any investment, Property values can fall as well as rise.

The authors offer this information as a guide only and it cannot be considered as financial advice in any way. Please refer to your independent financial advisor who is qualified to give you complete advice based on your circumstances.

The authors Rob Moore and Mark Homer are not qualified to give mortgage, legal or financial advice. Please seek legal and financial advice from a qualified advisor before making commitments. Neither its authors nor 'Progressive Property Ltd' accept liability for decisions made based on the content of this book.

Of course it was necessary to get that out of the way and it is something that you know already. This book is a guide and you have ultimate **choice** what you do or don't do with the content in these pages.

If you are looking for generic Property data and concepts, you need to read our first book "The 44 Most Closely Guarded Property Secrets."

If you are looking for MLM [Multi Level Marketing], get rich quick, zero to a million in 15 minutes, home based biz [£500 per month without having to work read from the back of a car or on a lamppost], or anything that says you'll make easy cash in your sleep in 5 minutes, then let us know when you find it and give us a piece!

But it doesn't happen like that for most people [we've never seen it] in our experience.

We don't want to waste your time. We know how valuable it is to you. We talk about it at length in this book and we`ll teach you to manage it well.

You can't get it back and how you use it will dictate your results, so use it well. Read this book more than once; you'll get far more from it and you'll see it from a different perspective each time.

And it will be **well worth your time.**

Section 2: Getting real

Denial

Most people are in denial about being in denial.

And the thing about being in denial is we don't actually know what is going on. In our business, in making money and in Property, awareness is fundamental. In both our books we stress the importance of testing and measuring and knowing exactly what your numbers are in your portfolio.

What is one of the main reasons why people don't succeed in Property? They try, they fail, they go bankrupt, they make some good decisions, but they still don't manage to make their portfolio work, and it's because they're in denial.

They're in denial either emotionally where they don't want to admit that they've made mistakes [most of the time those mistakes are necessary], they're not learning from their mistakes, or they just don't know what's going on because they're not measuring anything.

We've been in Property quite a few years now and what matters to us is *reality*. What matters to us is **what is actually happening** with our numbers, with our cashflow, with the equity and with the growth. Not some random calculation or marketing fluff based on what someone might tell us, or something that's happened in history, or something speculative, or a desktop valuation, or whatever.

It's all about reality.

We're going to run over with you the main things that people are in denial about, and how you can turn that around, keep a close eye on your portfolio, know your numbers, know the reality and therefore know for a fact that you're making money.

Cashflow

The biggest mistake that people make is they don`t keep a close enough eye on the cashflow of their properties. You will probably know that your rent versus your mortgage payments is not your only set of costs in your Property portfolio.

But of course most people see it that way. No honestly, they really do. We know it's totally insane, but it's denial. We all love the beaches and the sand and the white flowing clothes and the sun and the sea; but the flock are **dreaming about it**. They're in denial that results will happen out of thin air.

They believe that if the rent is £500 and the mortgage payments are £450, then that's a Property that cashflows at £50 a month. Or they have been lead to believe that and they haven't done their own diligence.

Now that's not you, but it **is** denial, because that's not the **reality**. Anyone who has had a Property 5 minutes knows that. If you ask anyone who's got a portfolio of 20+ properties, they will know that for an existing Property [older not new] you will need gas and boiler safety checks at around £88 a year, you need to pay a letting agent if you don't want to have all the pain of building and managing Property yourself [at between 10 and 15% per month].

Then you have average maintenance costs [we've averaged it out over our whole portfolio over a 5 year period and that, for us, works out at £213 a year]. Things are going to go wrong and things will need to be fixed.

There are lots of other costs too. If you buy a flat you need service charges such as ground rent and maintenance. There are insurances perhaps, there is bad debt [tenants not paying], there are voids. How long is your Property empty per month or per year as an average?

We've gone through our statistics and all of our data over the last 5 years and we know that 9.9 days per year every Property is empty. That's a fantastic number and we're still trying to get that down. Whatever it is, you need to know it.

Of course if we didn't do our numbers, and if we weren't looking at the reality of the situation through all of the spreadsheets and all of the data we've accrued, we would never know this.

You absolutely need to know this because you need to know what's going on. If there's a problem, you can put it right. **Fast** if you have to. But if you don't know what the problems are you can't solve them, and before you know it you won't be able to afford your portfolio anymore. This has happened so much over the last year with all the problems with new build properties.

People have bought Property; they believed it to be worth X when it was actually worth X minus 20%. They believed that the rent would be X when it was actually X minus 30%. They believed the cashflow to be X when it was actually X minus 30%. Because they didn't do their numbers [either upfront or while they we're going through the process of purchasing and renting], they didn't know what was going on until it was far too late.

Oh dear and ouch.

Discount

Most people [going back to 2001] who've been buying new Property, have been buying Property with discounts that aren't real. They are in denial.

They're in denial because they just believe what someone says to them without doing proper diligence, or having the relevant experience and knowledge that would bring it all out in the wash.

Now let's take this as an example: you want to sell a Property. Do you think that what you believe that Property is worth would be the same as what the person who's buying it believes it is worth?

Of course not. You're going to have bias and you're going to believe it's worth more than it really is because you're going to want to sell it for as much as possible, aren't you?

Nothing earth shattering there.

The buyer will have bias because they're going to think it's worth less than what you think it is worth, because they're going to want to buy it as cheaply as possible.

Makes sense.

Then there's an estate agent. Send an estate agent round a Property and what are they going to value it at? Good question. That's going to be different again because they may [in some instances] try to value it as high as possible so you'll list your Property with them over another agent. In some very cheeky instances we've seen [which we don't agree with], some estate agents will value it much lower to drop your expectation so maybe you'll consider selling it to them.

Already we have 4 different valuations of the same asset.

Then put the surveyor into the mix. What do they think that Property is worth? As little as possible to protect their personal liability is what the case usually is. These are all very different and we can all understand why there's great confusion [or opportunity; depends how you look at it]. It's all about perception. More later on perception and reality.

However, there is a way to find out exactly what your Property is worth. Look at all the comparable properties on comparable streets in comparable areas, and find out what they're on the market for, or what they're selling for: what the *market will pay for any given Property*.

You can get the asking prices from rightmove.co.uk. This is the best way to find out what Property is selling for. You can use the Land Registry for sold prices. You could also ask an estate agent what comparable properties have sold for. This is the best way to overcome denial.

The market is transient. Over a 6 month period your figures might not be 100% accurate [or static], but over a period of time you can get accurate figures on what your Property is worth based on other comparable properties. The great thing about existing Property, for example properties built in the 70's that are ex- Development Corporation, or long rows of terraced houses; **they're all the same**.

There are streets and streets of the same properties with the same layout, the same size, the same exterior, the same interior, the same garden and the same garage. You know that when one goes for £125,000 another one is worth £125,000. Even if there is a major difference inside to out it's probably only going to have £5,000 worth of difference.

That's how you understand **real value**.

Voids

Let's talk about voids because most people are in denial about voids. They'll tell you that this Property 'cashflows' at £50 a month or £200 a month or even in HMO examples [houses of multiple occupancy] you might be led to believe that properties will 'cashflow' at £350-£400, even £500 a month.

Now that sounds great doesn't it? We all want that please.

'I want no money down Property with no money in and cashflow and growth and zero maintenance and no time input!'

We're all obviously going to want a piece of that, but what the about reality?

So we decided to buy some HMOs in 2006/07. We bought 7 HMOs because there were so many people going on and on about 'cashflow 'and how much 'cashflow' you can make. In the end we were like 'right we're going to shut all of you lot up and we're going to buy a load'.

So we did.

We went slightly outside our strategy [our strategy is small, single let properties with high Council guaranteed rents with low void periods and high yields], but we have this attitude that you have to try things if you want a chance of them working.

We bought them and went along our merry way trying to rent them out. The reality is, [and bear in mind we've probably bought 100 properties for ourselves and investors in the last 12 months] that it takes much longer to rent those out than it does the single let properties. You're trying to find 5 tenants instead of one. One tenant could upset all the others, and suddenly you've got one or 2 or 3 empty rooms.

For that cashflow to happen you have to have all 5 rooms filled every day of the year, and the reality is that just didn`t happen. As soon as you have one room empty for a month or 2 your cashflow is gone with the wind.

When we put this through our spreadsheets and we accrued the data over the last 12-18 months we saw the reality: a lot of these supposedly cashflowing HMOs are actually shortfalling, sometimes up to £200 a month because you can't fill the rooms, there are much higher associated costs and because of the money you have to leave in the Property.

We're not saying that we were in denial. We trail-blazed it; we wanted to see what the reality was. But now we know the reality [or at least our reality based on our experience]. We know what we need to do about it;

we need to kick our letting agent up the backside, we need to get them to put the rents up, we need to get them to work harder and we need to get the rooms filled. In another year or 2 we'll get them cashflowing.

The reality is that voids will eat into your profit and if people assume [which nearly everyone does], that cashflow is based on a Property renting out every day of the year, well that's just not going to happen. You need to know the number of days, as an average, that your properties are vacant every single month and every single year.

This section is so important because, although we all want to go and make money and that's great and yeah we know we're going to get growth for the next infinite amount of years and over the next 7-10 years our portfolios are going to double in value...

Yes we all know that.

But if we can't get the cashflow right from day one then there's a very good chance, especially when you upscale and you build your portfolio to 20, 50,100, 200 properties, that negative cashflow could kill you.

Just £50 [gross] shortfall probably means £300 [net] a month on a Property; well that's manageable, isn't it? Times that by 10 and that's £3,000 a month, times that by another 10 and that's £30,000 a month you've got to find. Not many people will want to do that.

Summary

Most people are in denial about being in denial. Don't assume anything. Do your diligence and research, be clear on your strengths and weaknesses and go into Property as informed as you can. You are responsible for making yourself rich and successful. Be honest with yourself.

Time [wasting]

In our first book, "The 44 Most Closely Guarded Property Secrets" we devoted one whole secret and one whole section to time and how *time is your most precious commodity*. We're going to expand on that in this book and make it more relevant to how you can make money in the Property market right now.

When we study unsuccessful people, lazy people, people who are running around like blue arsed flies but aren't achieving anything, people who talk the best game but play the worst game or people who just aren't getting the results they believe they deserve, there is one common underlying theme every single time. Now there may be other factors but my experience of coaching people over the last 4 years [Rob] has found that they are spending most of their time in the wrong places.

Facebook, MSN, the Nintendo DS and Big Brother.

They either don't know where they're spending their time [they are doing things habitually through bad training] or they do know where they're spending their time but are choosing to spend it in the areas that don't generate them money or results now. It's not all about money, but you're reading this book because you want to make money in Property right now, aren't you?

And you can set up the rest of your life in the rest of this year if you *use your time wisely*.

You absolutely need to keep a time log of where you use your time. It might sound a bit strange; a bit anal perhaps, but stick with us because it is vital. If you don't measure where you use your time, then you'll guess. When you guess what you do [and this is what we all do] you'll be naturally biased. You'll wear your rose tinted glasses and you'll say to yourself something like:

'Yeah I spend 6 hours a day researching Property, when in fact you probably spend one hour a day on actual research and 5 hours on the Property section of Facebook who are friends who happen to like Property too.

Now we know this isn't you, but...

We have to get real and tough with ourselves here. The way I've done it over the last few years [Rob] is I've kept a time log on a word document that stays open on one of my 3 computer screens all day every day. I'm strict with myself [because no one else will be. My girlfriend tells me what to do but that's only after office hours!].

Every hour in my working day gets logged on the word doc, it only takes 5 minutes a day, and it shows me where I've used my time.

You have to be honest with yourself, and if you've been on Facebook for 2 hours, then write it down.

Of course you can use that data to study and improve. It's like when you go on a diet. What do personal trainers always tell you to do?
They tell you to make a note or a diary of the things that you're eating. How else can they help you if they don't know what you're putting in your stomach? If you're eating cakes and chocolate bars and everything else in

the Smeg but you say that you're eating low fat muffins and Greek natural yoghurt, then of course you're results aren't going to be consistent.

The second important step is to stop doing things that don't get you the results you want. If you read our first book "The 44 Most Closely Guarded Property Secrets" then you will now know, or have a good idea, of the results you want.

MySpace, MSN, Facebook, Big Brother and having 3 hour meetings that could take 15 minutes *don't increase your bottom line*. They don't get you the results you'll want. They're not going to make you money. They're not going to build assets for you. They're not going to set your family free. They're not going to give you the lifestyle you want. They're not going to buy you your Ferrari. They're not going to buy you your shoes and handbags.

So what you need to ascertain in terms of time is the following very important question:

'What is it that I can do that will generate money?'

Work out what it is and do more of it. And then more and more. We talk about how you can do that specifically later.

Another reason why people don't spend enough of their time in areas that make them the most money is [and this is the biggest one by far] that it might not be *comfortable* for them. What might be comfortable for them is to do what they've always done.

It might be painful, it might be boring and they may have to concentrate or do something that they are not immediately good at.

But of course if you do what you've always done then you'll get the same results as you've always got. You'll remember from our last book what Einstein said about the definition of insanity.

Sometimes it's not that comfortable to spend your time doing the things that make money. But of course you know that you have to push yourself out of your comfort zone, into a position that is 'challenging' [otherwise known as opportunity].

In Property what makes the money is researching the area, what makes the money is doing the viewings, what makes the money is putting in the offers, what makes the money is making sure the solicitors work well together, what makes the money is getting the best mortgage products, what makes the money is getting the properties tenanted quickly, what makes the money is buying the right properties at the right price.

To do all of those you need to understand sales, you need to understand negotiation and you need to understand marketing [and you need to feel confident enough to put this knowledge into practice]. They might not sound comfortable to you yet; they certainly didn't to us a few years ago, but the fact remains that everything else you do will probably generate about 5% of your money, and that's where most people spend 80% of their time [because it's easy for them]. This is the exact reason why most people don't get the results they want!

Genius discovery eh?!

If you just turn that on its head and spend 80% of your time in the areas that do *make you money*, and in those areas we've just mentioned, you will phenomenally change the amount of money that you make in Property right now.

That's the 80/20 principle [later in this section].

Let us give you another example of time, and where it's used wisely [or unwisely]. We speak to people so regularly at meetings, events, open days and seminars that say:

'There is no way you can get 30% below market deals.'

So that's end of story then, isn't it?! Let's all go home and give up now, what time is Big Brother on?

Having read our first book you immediately know the reason they're not finding the deals is because they don't believe they can find the deals. Because they don't believe they can find the deals they don't look for the deals. Because they don't look for the deals they don't find the deals.

Take a breath for a minute!

And while you do, here is a little story about belief. Have you ever tried to catch fleas in a jar? Us neither, it's pretty sad and you need good eyesight and little fingers. However fleas are very habitual, just like us. This is another true story about fellow inhabitants of our planet that act like us [and we're supposed to be the most intelligent of all the species]!

If you were to catch fleas in a jar, they would jump and jump [like they do], banging their head on the lid of the jar as they try and jump to freedom. They'll do it over and over and over, expecting the same result [they should have had a chat with Einstein].

You can take the lid off the jar once you've stopped teasing them, so that they can jump one last time to freedom. The interesting thing is that, despite the opportunity, they will continue to jump to the same height that they had been jumping to when the lid was on, over and over and over.

You give them the chance of freedom and they don't take it. Something to think about there. They have set their ceiling, and once set, they find it very difficult to break through that ceiling.

People are exactly the same with their beliefs. They set their ceiling, [most probably unconsciously], and that is it. They don't believe that they can achieve anything higher than that ceiling.

Fundamental tip no.1:
You have to raise your own ceiling of belief every day to get the results you think you want.

Because people believe they can't find deals that are out there, they don't. It's people like us, and you, who find the deals. So their truth is their reality as they see it; it's the Expectation theory [next chapter: and it's a good one]. Their ceiling is the highest point that they'll get to.

To get a good understanding of this, talk to someone who earns £20,000 per year and then to someone who earns £100,000 a year. Their beliefs around what they can earn, spend and what they can achieve will be very different.

The reason that we can buy 30% below market value Property [we know this because we've done it so many times, and we know so many other people who have done the same] is because we are spending a bigger proportion of our time on the people or places that are likely, or are most likely from our research, to sell us the Property at the price we want to pay.

And because we expect it to happen.

What most people do wrong is that they spend too much of their time on what we call 'unmotivated sellers.' Sellers who aren't going to sell the Property at a discount because they're not motivated enough. Simple. They want the best price and *they don't need to sell* it any cheaper. So many people spend all of their time on 'unmotivated sellers' when the fact of the matter remains, you can establish in 5 minutes whether someone's motivated by asking a script of questions [are they going through probate, a divorce, are they relocating, do they have debt problems?], all of which will be *given to you in this book*.

There are all manner of things that make someone 'motivated' to sell based on time, speed and trust way, way above price on their list of priorities. They're the people you want to find.

Summary

Stop messing about with things that don't get you the results you want. Get real with yourself, only you can control your time. Keep a work log and become an expert planner, and your wealth will increase exponentially.

Expectation theory

Anyone who decides to be the black Sheep, who decides that they don't want to go with the flock, will realise that at this time, [and we mean **right now** in this time] there is huge opportunity.

When people believe they have lost money, they'll lose money. When people believe that their Property has gone down, then they'll think to themselves 'I'm going to sell this because I've lost money.'

But of course selling the Property makes them lose the money [they wouldn't have lost it had they not sold it] and it's the belief that they were losing money that made them lose the money. That's a bit of a tongue twister but this is a hugely important **fact**.

There is a well known economic phenomenon that's called the 'Expectations Theory.' This is it perfectly at work. Like Art. Now this is really, really interesting. It's interesting that we can put an economic 'theory' on what we see happen all the time. Not just in the Property market, not just in the stock market or anything to do with money, but in everyday life.

In the Property market, when you get a 'boom bust' scenario; when a 'boom' [bull market] leads to a 'bust' [bear market], it's not always just because of what is actually happening in the economy or what the reality is, it's very often **driven by sentiment**.

Because people expect a 'bust' [crash] now after the boom for the last 7 or 8 years, [not necessarily because it's going to happen or that it is the reality] then that's actually what starts to happen.

Rob Moore & Mark Homer

The market is driven as much by sentiment as it is by what is actually happening, **because perception becomes reality.** This [again] is the Sheep mentality perfectly explained. People will start to sell Property when they believe a 'bust' is imminent or that the market's going down, because they'll try and second guess that the market's going to go down even further.

Fear sells newspapers and gets TV ratings. Fear causes people to make irrational [emotional] decisions.

And of course this catches on and this persuades the masses [Baa] to do likewise [follow the Sheep]. This leads to a massive rush to sell, and all of a sudden the market experiences a drop or a 'crash.'

Without panic nothing happens.

We used to hate all this, because we just kept trying to tell everyone that they're all wrong. We now realise that we need the masses to act like this. We need the statistics to be like they are so that we [as non average; professional contrarian investors] can make serious profit.

Of course this thought process [some might say 'phenomenon'] can be applied to your own thought process, your investment strategy and your ability to **make money right now in this Property market** crash. Not just because you want to eradicate this thinking from your mindset, but also because when you can see this happening, you know what is happening based on the psychology of sheople; and you know what they're going to do.

If you know that we're in a buyer's market where not many people are buying [because everyone is in fear and is selling] you can create opportunity as a buyer if you're liquid [cash] or even if you're not [you can borrow a mountain of cash].

It's not always easy to be the black Sheep. It's not always easy to have *that much confidence in yourself* that when 99% are going one way, you're going to decisively go the other way. And that's why it's *only the 1% that make all the money*.

Summary

You get what you expect. It is a scientifically proven phenomenon. Expect the results that you desire, and you'll get them. Expect what 99% of people get, and you'll get what 99% of people get. Markets are driven by expectation and not necessarily by reality. Understand this and use it to chip away at Property prices.

But I can't do that!

At every seminar we speak at, every meeting we have, every time we write an article in a major publication, every time we appear on TV, we always come across people who believe that what can be achieved in Property, they can't do. It won't work for them.

For whatever reason [unimportant], they have their limiting beliefs that hold them back. Maybe it was because they were too much like their father, or maybe they didn't go to university, or maybe they're too busy or maybe they've got 3 kids.

Every time we talk about focus; buying in one specific area, we get 'but I can't do that, I live in London and the prices are far too expensive'.

Look harder. Move out a little further out [Essex, Milton Keynes], raise more money, get the necessary knowledge, meet the people who can help you.

Fundamental tip no.2:
There's always an answer if you're looking for a solution rather than focusing on the problem.

When we tell people that we're getting yields of 8%+ we get 'yes but I can't get yields of 8% because I invest in London and the yields are 4%.' Let us tell you this; there are still properties in London that are worth £150,000, and you can find them if you're looking.

When people are focused on the problem that's what they'll find and that's what they'll continue to get; they won't find the solution.

Rob Moore & Mark Homer

There will always be the 'yes but' people: yes that sounds good but; yes that sounds good but; yes that sounds good but...

They are problem focused people; they're looking for the obstacles and hurdles and of course they find them and hit them [hard]. They're just looking to say:

'Oh wait a minute I told you that wouldn't work. I knew I wouldn't be able to do that, every time I try to do something it never goes right.'

That's their reality, that's what they will get because they choose to focus on those things. *That doesn't have to be your reality.* You have ultimate choice. Being solution focused is a totally different mindset. Just being open to opportunity will lead you down a path that you never expected to take. When we started in Property we never believed that 1, 2 or 5 years down the line we'd have written books, been on TV shows, been in major newspaper publications commenting on Property and being told that we're experts. But of course every single opportunity that we see, every problem that we look at and look to find the solution to, that's what we find in the end.

Throughout this book your unconscious mind may say 'yes but.'

'You're buying Property 30% below market value, yes but.'

'You're getting yields of 8 or 9%, yes but.'

'You're getting cash flow, growth and equity from purchase, yes but.'

'Yes but on Saturdays I have to see my children.'

'Yes but I work 60 hours a week.'

That's fine. Some of the most successful Property investors have come from jobs that were 60 hours a week, some of the most successful Property investors have 3 children, some of the most successful Property investors are women [don't even try to use that one girls!], and some of the most successful Property investors were £30,000, £50,000, £100,000+ in debt before they got into Property.

But something triggered them to do it. Perhaps it was a decision they made or perhaps they were fortunate and something fell into their lap. Something triggered them to make them realise that **Property works**. As long as you understand that Property works and you've sold yourself on the concept that Property works [only you can do that], then every 'yes but' should be able to be answered.

Summary

Always finding reasons, stories and excuses why you can't do something will give you what you've always got. Instead of finding a story or an excuse, successful people find an answer.

Simple vs. easy

Since 2001, there have been many companies and one-man bands who have marketed to normal people the fact that Property investment is easy. You can make money easily, you can make money when you're asleep, you can make money with your eyes shut, you can make money standing on your head, you can make money in your dreams.

All you have to do is buy Property and you will be a Squillionaire. Zero to a million in 5 minutes.

They market pictures of their Ferraris and they show you pictures of their watches and cufflinks and their fancy ties, and they would have you believe that investing in Property and becoming a millionaire is easy.

This is an absolute myth. This is bullshit.

At least it is from our own personal experience. We got attracted into the Property market by this type of marketing. We don't have a fear or an aversion to this type of marketing. We are grateful that they made it sound so easy so that we **took the first and most important step**; we got into Property.

However our **reality** was very different.

Consider this: would any company marketing their services say: 'Well Property isn't that easy, it's actually quite difficult and this is what will happen; you'll think it's really easy and you'll buy a few properties, you won't know what to do, it will cause you a lot of pain, you'll lose some money before you make any, you'll look like an idiot, you might even get divorced, it will cause you some grief but if you stick at it in the long run, in 5 or 10 years you will make money. You'll learn a lot, you'll become tough, you'll become strong, you won't make the mistakes you did and ultimately down the line you can earn enough money passively so that you don't have to work. Realistically within 5 to 10 years you might be a millionaire but only one in 100 actually will in reality!'

If they market like that who do you think would buy their products? You got it: no one!

This section is very, very important and it's come at the start of the book because we want to *get real with you* right now. Let's not kid each other here. You're going to like us much more for it in the end. You are going to appreciate that we told you the reality and you will be far better prepared for what you are about to undertake.

Property is not easy; there will be difficulties, there will be challenges, but there will be opportunities if you can stick it out. There will be things you'll have to do that you don't know yet, that you don't understand yet, and you'll have to go through some challenges to understand how to do them.

Once you've learned what to do things become easier. Walking is easy for most of you now but it wasn't always easy. Imagine your Mum and Dad saying, 'oh well, he's not gonna be a walker,' after you fall on your face for the first time! Riding a bike is easy for you now but it wasn't always easy. You probably got a few grazes and bruises learning to ride.

However, Property investment, just like everything else, is simple. The difference between being simple and easy is essential to understand.

If something is simple, like Property investing, someone can give you a blueprint, someone can give you the 44 Secrets, or a list of all the things you need to do, and you can go out and follow those blueprints and secrets and you'll get to where you want to be.

Providing that you do them and you don't give up.

If they're nice they'll also give you a few warnings. They'll pre-empt some mistakes that other people have made and they'll inform you of the challenges you are likely to experience. You'll get a blueprint that starts at the start, and takes you to the end, much like a map.

If you follow that blueprint, you will succeed, at least to the degree of the person who gave you the blueprint. Then you go out and get a new one to take you to your next level. The most successful and wealthy people in the world understand this concept. You should follow these concepts. If you do to the letter [to the Law] in the most simple and dumbed down way, step by step, just like reading a manual or a set of instructions, then you will become wealthy in Property.

Your goals are personal to you and how wealthy you want to become. How much involvement you want to have will be down to you. But know this: Property investment is not easy [because we'd all be loaded], but it is simple.

Summary

There's a world of difference between simple and easy. Easy is not the reality for most people, but simple can be. Follow a set of rules and guidelines and don't give up, and you will get to where you want to be. Simple [but not easy!]

80/20 principle [or 95/5, or 99/1]

You probably know the 80/20 principle [or Pareto's Law] that states that 80% of results [both universally and personally applicable] are achieved from 20% of the total time input.

80% of the money is made by 20% of the people, 80% of your money is made in 20% of your time and 80% of your happiness is gained in 20% of the things that you do.

This is the most amazing phenomenon that we've ever learned because it applies to everything: 80% of the wear in the carpet is in 20% of the area, 80% of the food you eat is in 20% of the time, 80% of your golf shots are taken by 20% of your clubs and 80% of your handbags and shoes make up only 20% of the usage!

We've never known anything like. This is **the Law**. This is the Bible that we live by at Progressive. Just think about it for a second. If we all spend 80% of our time getting 20% of our results, then 80% of our results come from 20% of our time.

Just being aware of it makes a huge difference. And so it should be really easy to flip that on its head and improve our results 5-fold, shouldn't it?!

Well no!

80% of the wealth in the world is owned by just a few people [funnily enough, by around 20%]. Even more interesting is that if you take that 20%, you can apply the same Law again: 80% of the wealth in the 20% bracket is held by 20% of the people [4% out of the 100].

Rob Moore & Mark Homer

And so it continues...

In our previous book "The 44 Most Closely Guarded Property Secrets" we explain the Laws of compounding and attraction. Now if you haven't read the book or you don't understand those yet, you might want to go to:

www.progressiveproperty.co.uk/book-buy-now

These Laws state that you get more of what you already have and you attract more of what you have already into your life. That's why money attracts money, because the more you have the more you attract. The Law of compounding states that the more money you have and the more money you invest, the more money you earn [on a growing amount of money].

These Laws aren't just applicable to Property; they form the basis of psychology as well. And like Expectation theory, it can be used to your advantage, because you will get what you expect. That's 100% a fact.

So if you can be strong enough in these times with a clear strategy and some clear rules [which we'll talk about later on in detail in the book], then now is the best time. Believe us when we tell you that **right now is the best time for you** to make money, for you to buy Property at 30% below market value. This is something that we've been doing now since we saw the market turn in September 2007, and we believe that this is going to continue; and this is why we've **written this book right now**.

And you know what? In 2 years this book might not be as relevant, but right now this is the book that you want to read if you want to make cash in the Property market.

Let us also tell you this: in 5 years we genuinely believe [this is our prediction] that people will be talking about what happened in 2008. You'll have most of the 'sheople,' [99% of people] telling stories of when they sold and how they lost money. How everything cost so much, how they had no money to spend and how the government are eeeeeeeevil.

But 1% of people will be saying how they bought 10, 20 or 50, properties in 2008/9. They bought them all with no money, they bought them all at 18-30% below market value and those properties have doubled in 5 years. Now we won't know if we're right until 5 years time, and we all love a prediction, but we genuinely believe that's going to happen based on what we've seen happen over history, and what we've learned from all the mentors that we've ever studied [and how they've made a huge amount of their money in Property].

Summary

80% of your results are achieved using 20% of your time. It is Pareto's Law and it seems to apply to everything you do. 80% of the wealth lies in the hands of 20% of the people. How can you use your time wisely to get 500% [5 times as much] of your results using 80% of your time? Facebook, MSN and non IGT tasks are where most people spend 80% of their time, and they get the results to show for it.

Averages [as a guide only please]

If it is the historical fact that properties double in value every 7-10 years on average that got you into Property, then that's fantastic. If it's the fact that in your area your properties grow at the national average of 10% per year that got you into Property, then that's fantastic.

Averages are definitely a good gauge from a conceptual point of view to help you understand a general overview of the type of investment you're going into. If the average yield for the properties that you buy in your area is 7% and it's that that gets you investing in Property then that's also fantastic.

Let us also tell you something about averages and the myth of averages:

Averages are only really relevant for statistical purposes for the media, for newspapers, for spin, for hype, for arguments, for evidence to back up an article or a statement, and for your overall peace of mind at any one given point in time.

Think about it for a minute. The 'average' growth for the UK in 2007 is not really relevant if you invest in Peterborough. Surely what's most relevant for you is the growth that you receive in Peterborough. Growth in Lands End is pretty irrelevant to you.

Surely what the 'average' Property investor does or what the market grows as an 'average' is not particularly relevant to you because our guess is that you don't view yourself as Mr. or Mrs. Average. That, by definition, would put you in the 80% or the 99% [where average people are], and why would you want to be in there? You're reading this book for a reason, aren't you?

Surely you're going to be expecting results that are better than average; and you should.

Average statistics are certainly useful for marketing, they're certainly a good gauge for what's happening overall, and we would expect that you would be **more successful than the 80% [or the 99%] of Property investors out there**. 99% of them fit into the speculative investor category rather than the professional, serious, seasoned, skilful, and knowledgeable investor category.

So knowing that properties double in value every 7-10 years as an average across the UK now; do you think it's possible that you could beat that average?

Absolutely. And if you don't, you won't!

You should be thinking to yourself right now that you are going to beat that average. You might say:

'Well yes but if that's the average then some places don't perform as well as the average, and some places perform better than the average.'

Correct. Having read these 2 books and being committed and focused; persevering, getting the knowledge, doing the analysis, all of these things that you do [that 99%of people don't do], should put you into that 1%. It is the 1% that get better than average growth, better than average yield, better than average cashflow, better than average ROI, better than average results and a better than average lifestyle.

The point of this section is to get you to think realistically about what you can achieve. We would suggest that realistically you can achieve the national averages for yield and growth and everything else just by being average. Think about this for a minute now...

Locations vary significantly. From London to Leeds the results, growth, cashflow and yield can vary immensely. In Peterborough we're buying studio flats for £50,000 that are worth £75,000 on the open market. You can't buy a garage in some parts of London for £50,000, so £50,000 certainly isn't the average price, but that £50,000 Property will give you way better than average yield, way better than average growth, lower than average maintenance, lower than average ground rent, better than average cashflow and has a far higher than average amount of equity in it.

Yes you might say 'well you're fortunate you live in a good area, I don't live in a good area.' It wouldn't be the first time we've heard that, would it? Or how about this one: 'you guys were lucky, you got into Property at just the right time!'

Well actually no. When we moved to Peterborough we didn't know that Property was going to be so lucrative here. We didn't get into Property 20 years ago; our portfolio would be worth about £500million by now if we had.

But of course 5 years of study, listening to mentors, persevering when people were telling us that Property was a stupid idea at the time, or that we've missed the boat, or that we're too young, or that we don't know enough or that we don't have enough money.

We persevered, we had disdain for the average, and 4 years later we're getting discounts of 30% [£25,000 off £75,000 properties, £35,000 off £130,000 properties], a discount that 2 years ago we would've struggled to believe we could get, let alone achieve. A discount that is **anything but average**.

But of course that's the reality right now because we're much better than we were last year and we'll be getting better every year. We **refuse to be average**. The market has changed and we're aware how different things are now, and we're utilising every single one of the things that is mentioned in this book. That's not what 'average' people do. We believe in you and refuse to believe that you are average too.

Summary

The Law of averages is for average people. Use averages for statistical use but don't set your strategy in stone based on national averages. Your research will show that you can outperform the average with increased knowledge.

The myth of competition

The reason most people give up [simple vs. easy] is because they either believe it should be easy or they've been marketed to and made to believe it is easy. As they hit the first hurdle they realise 'ouch that wasn't easy, that hurt, OK, I'm going to give up.'

Most people will find 50 or 100 reasons and excuses; talking themselves out of doing something, just so they've got a story to tell of why they didn't succeed. Whatever makes them happy!

Competition is a myth. Using the 80/20 principle we talk about many times in this book, at least 80%, or 99/1 [99%] of the competition in any market isn't in fact competition, because they don't know what they're doing.

Owner-occupiers aren't investors, 'speculative' investors aren't investors; only professional investors are really investors *making Property work and making it profitable*. You don't really have to compete with owner-occupiers and speculative investors because [just by reading these books] you'll be better than them.

The only people you need to 'compete' with are professional investors, and of course they make up a very small percentage of the market numerically. Most people talk themselves out of even starting and say:

'Oh you know you can't get any deals off estate agents in Peterborough because Mark and Rob are getting them all!'

Well maybe we are getting a lot but everyone starts somewhere, and you will only be competing with a select few people. We're only competing with 2 other people in the market at the moment for buying Property. If we believed in competition, we'd probably talk ourselves out of even starting. That would be a £4million+ mistake!

Everyone else believes in the myth of competition; they'll try and they'll make a mistake [if they get that far], they'll hit their first hurdle, and they won't carry on. Using Google Adwords to try to find leads to buy properties: most of the people you're competing with are spending too much money, they're bidding far too high, the quality of their ads and their pages are poor, they don't direct you to the right pages [which aren't optimised], they don't understand calls to action, benefit driven headlines, eye mapping, they don't understand what they're doing and they're spending a load of money.

That's not your competition! Why would you use such a poor strategy? Why would you be so average?!

You have to start somewhere and *wherever you're at right now is perfect* and right where you should be. Do not let the myth of competition stop you from making money because *most people aren't making any money and they're not your competition.*

Summary

Competition exists mostly in your head. 95% of your competition is not your competition because they aren't doing it right. The other 5% are, so all you need to do is find them and copy what they do. Most people use competition as an excuse to give up or stay on the sofa watching Big Brother.

Section 3: The current market

Long term vision, short term opportunity

In our first book "The 44 Most Closely Guarded Property Secrets" one of the secrets was thinking mid to long term. For your overall vision and strategy, for building wealth or building a huge Property portfolio to make cash, for freedom, choice, happiness and independence, having a long term plan will absolutely make sure that you get there [and not having one will have the opposite effect].

In fact it will normally make sure that you'll get there quicker than having a 'short term focused' view on wealth and on the market in general. We don't want to cover the long term strategy in this book because we've already covered it in our last book. What we do want to mention is that your long term view is very important because you don't win a marathon sprinting for a mile.

You just get knackered and have to give up before the end.

But of course sprinting for a mile could set you up for victory in the marathon, if timed well. Long term is really important in terms of putting your flag in the ground so that you have a target which you can shoot for.

The flag can move, and that's OK, but you need to know where you're going in order for you to start your journey.

The short term aspect of this particular section of the book is relevant right now. Next year, this short term plan may change; it might work a little, it might not work at all.

For you to be able to buy Property at 18-30% below market value, you need to be liquid; you need to be able to act and decide very, very quickly; you have to act with conviction; you have to accept that the deals that are around today may not be around tomorrow; you need to accept that the lending that's around today might not be around tomorrow.

Let's run over them again because they are so important [Now]:

1. You need to be liquid [access to cash fast]
2. Act and decide very quickly
3. Act with conviction
4. Accept that deals here today could be gone tomorrow
5. Accept that lending is changing fast

There's huge opportunity in the short term, and once you find something that works, once you find a strategy that you can replicate, you need to act quickly. Hammer and bang out and repeat and go for it. But understand that this won't last forever and it will change.

Yes your long term view of the Property market will make money; approximately every 7-10 years your portfolio will double. There is an opportunity right now for you to make 30% of that 100% growth in 5 minutes flat in the purchase of just one Property.

Times that by 5 or 10. Then compound it.

Opportunity like this has never ever existed in the whole time we've personally been in the market. People we've spoken to who have been in the market for 30 years have never experienced what we're experiencing today. The likelihood is that this may only happen once every 10 years, if we're lucky!

Accelerate your 7-10 year growth plan now by buying Property at 30% below market value; you've just made one third of that growth in the purchase of that one Property. Why wait 5 years to take another 5 years to do it?!

Of course Property may continue to fall but at some point it's going to start growing, and with 30% equity from day one, you could experience your portfolio doubling in 5 years, or even less. It's not unheard of for professional investors to double their portfolio value in 3 years.

Social proof: it's been done before; it can be done again [more about that later].

90% of this is mindset, and relies on you being decisive, focused, strong in your convictions, not listening to the Sheep and not being clawed back by the Crabs.

Summary

Your Property wealth building plan is a long term strategy, and you will make cash in the long term to create your life of choice for you, and for generations to come. Understand also that the opportunity to buy cheaply and make real cash is in the market right now. You could make 3 years growth in one deal. Times that by 5 or 10 and you'll have an asset base that will look after you for life.

Understanding a buyers' market

This is fundamental in your ability to make vast amounts of Property cash right now and in certain 'pockets' of time in the future. The definition of a buyers' market is:

'A market that is more in favour of buyers because there are more sellers than buyers in the market. Buyers control price because of a lack of liquidity and competition.'

Lack of liquidity

Currently lending is a lot more difficult than it used to be. Banks are not lending to each other as easily they are lending at higher rates and there is a lack of trust and confidence between financial institutions. Look at the recent interbank lending rates [libor and euribor] and you will see this reflected in the figures [on the next page].

Therefore most buyers have stopped buying. Fear and uncertainty are paralysing. Most people would rather wait than act. Rabbit in the headlights.

Now because of this, a lot of banks aren't liquid [no cash]; banks that don't have high street branches and don't have a lot of cash from savers who deposit cash. Not all banks are like your high street varieties: Barclays, Nationwide, Royal Bank of Scotland, The Halifax and so on who have many high street branches, many savers and depositors, and are very 'liquid.'

Many of the lenders [mortgage companies] that are relevant for you don't have high street branches and rely on lending money to you that's been loaned to them by other banks [with liquidity]. This has really reduced the lending in the market and the statistics back this up. According to the CML [Council of mortgage lenders] lending in the market is down almost 40% on last year.

If the banks are lending to each other, they are at such a high rate that this just gets passed on to the investor and owner occupier. Here is an article from The Guardian:

'The global credit crunch appeared to take a fresh turn for the worse today as interbank lending rates, known as Libor, rose to new two-month highs in London and the eurozone.

Interbank interest rates are set by the demand and supply of money rather than the Bank of England, and analysts say the latest rates signal a tightening of supply.

The sterling three-month Libor rate rose to 5.77%, more than 50 basis points above the Bank of England's 5.25% base rate – its highest level for two months.

The euro three-month Libor rose to its highest level since mid-January, standing at 4.39%.'

If you look at the Libor rate of 5.77% you can see that once the rates are then passed on to us, they will be much higher than that. Lending rates to actual investors were lower than that 9 months ago.

The statistics and the press also suggest that there are just not many people who can obtain finance:

Here is an article from the Times Online:

'In the past 2 months, the average time it takes to sell a Property has risen sharply. In greater London, it is no longer 2 weeks but 3; in Wales, it is 9 and a half – 3 times as long as it was just 9 weeks ago. "London has put a gloss on the figures for the past 12 months," says Richard Donnell, Hometrack's director.

"Prices have been driven by a shortage of stock and strong demand. Now that this is no longer the case, the froth is coming off. Because they cannot obtain finance they can't buy Property and that reduces the number of buyers in the market.'

Sharp increase in Property prices

An additional factor that has implications on people's ability to buy is the huge surge of growth since 2001 over and above the natural, average growth curve.

Property prices up until 2007 have been very high and because of that your average person, Joe or Jo; your first time buyer or owner-occupier, cannot afford [even if they could get lending] to buy Property. They have been out-priced in the market so that reduces another large percentage of the buying market.

You're not actually left with that many people after this!

The economy

Public spending is going down, there's not much confidence in the economy, the Expectation theory has filtered through the news and the papers and we're experiencing huge increases in the cost of living.

Even people who do have cash are thinking they don't want spend it at the moment just in case things get worse. Flock mentality and fear. Expectation theory. Caution. Low risk. They don't want to borrow cash either so they just hold tight. They wait and they don't do anything.

This has huge implications on the whole market. Nearly all of the buyers are gone: buyers' market. There are still as many sellers out there as normal, in fact it has even been reported by some publications that there are in fact more sellers than normal. Refer back to the quote on the previous page.

People still need to sell. The market doesn't just roll over and die with its paws in the air all rigid and everyone stops selling. Many people still need to sell, regardless of market conditions. People are still motivated.

There are even more sellers because people are panicking and want [or need] to sell. They **think they have to sell**. All hell and panic breaks loose, anarchy and looting and Baa Baa Click Click.

To have a 'balanced market' you need to have as many buyers as sellers. But when you're in a buyers' market there are more sellers because there are more people who want to get out, liquidate, sell up or cash in [or take a loss to prevent a bigger loss] this time because they're worried.

But wait a second; there are so few buyers out there who will buy their house. At the moment it's the same if you're trying to sell anything. That gives the buyer the advantage and 'negotiation power.'

I [Mark] have recently bought a new Car. The Car that I wanted to buy for the summer was selling on Auto Trader [3 years old] at about £30,000. Knowing what I know about the Property market and the economy, and enjoying a deal of course, I was never going to pay list price.

I have viewed quite a few and have probably been a bit more analytical than I might normally, but it's an opportunity for me to test my skills and save some money. I made quite a few very low offers and *had total negotiation power* because no one could sell them. In the end I bought the Car I wanted with all £1,000's of additional extras for £25,000.

If you go on Auto Trader now you can buy 4 or 5 year old Range Rovers for £15,000. They are £70,000 new. That says a lot about residual values and the impact that the economy [and petrol prices] is having on the resale markets.

At the moment in Peterborough [our patch], there are only 2 other buyers that we're competing against regularly. We're normally competing with 10, 11, sometimes up to 15 reasonably pro-active 'investors' in our town at any one time. That's gone down to 2 in the space of 3 months.

But what about all the people who still need to sell? Where do you think the power lies now? It puts the power in our hands. We're able to buy so much cheaper because there is far less competition and sellers cannot play buyers against each other. They cannot pick and choose. They can't be patient and wait for another buyer with a better offer to come along, because there aren't any!

Therefore we can reduce our offers. That's what we've been experiencing on a daily basis through April, May and June 2008. We are able to control the price that we buy Property for because people are hugely motivated at the moment.

People are hugely motivated because they're panicking, they're worried and they're scared. They have the fear of loss of more money because they [have been indoctrinated to] think that the market is going to continue to go down and down and down to 50% of its value. They want to get out right now because they don't want to lose any more money.

These are huge emotional drivers that will cause people to make irrational decisions.

They can't see the long term.

You've probably experienced it in your own house. You may have read the nationwide statistics. Just ask your Dad or your aunt what they bought their properties for way back when!

When we run our open days we are continually surprised by the amount of *money people have made accidentally*. We have had many people make 300% growth in less than 10 years. Most people have made 200% growth in 5 to 8 years.

You know that if people took the long term view they wouldn't lose any money. But of course these emotional based factors make people do illogical things and cause bad financial decisions.

And of course, some people have gotten into such a bad financial state that they have no other choice; they are **even more motivated**. This is what you will need to understand right now and use to your advantage in this market. If you are in a position where you are reasonably liquid [access to cash or finance] then you will hold the negotiation power and will be in a position to buy Property at heavily discounted prices. You can read more about motivated sellers in section 5.

Your belief that you can buy Property really cheaply should increase in this time because **people are physically buying Property that is much cheaper**. It is something that you will see with your own eyes [as long as they are open]. If you're one of these people who need the evidence then the evidence is in here. If you don't need the evidence then you just need to understand that because you are one of very few buyers around at this time, you can reduce your offers right down now.

At the moment with lending as it is [tough and scrappy] rents have to work [cover the mortgage by up to 130%, 30% up on last year] so you need to offer lower anyway to make the deals work; just to get finance.

The fact that mortgage companies are increasing their rates almost weekly and making it more difficult for us to borrow gives you more leverage to offer even lower. They are pushing the percentage of rental income that's needed up and increasing the amount of deposit that you need. You have no choice but to offer lower. This acts as a negotiation tool.

You won't even obtain finance unless you buy really cheaply. So everything at the moment is geared towards buying Property [cheaply], not selling. There really is no excuse for buying a Property that's any worse than 18% below the current market value.

A seller's market occurs when there are more buyers in the market than sellers. That's not rocket science, is it? The sellers control the market; they can be more selective over the price at which they want to sell their Property, because they know that there are lots of buyers out there who will compete to buy those properties. They know they can pick and choose and that the buyers will get into some kind of eBay bidding frenzy syndrome and fight and scrap and get emotional and buy far too high. Speculative investors often do this in between stages of the market cycles because they are always a little too late.

We explain market cycles later in this section.

This is basic economics; the law of supply and demand. As you get a greater supply, the demand [or the price at which you can sell something] reduces, and vice versa. We were in more of a sellers' market in 2007 because we were still experiencing good amounts of growth.

Your average Jo or Joe has been waiting and waiting and waiting. Eventually people are going to get on this bandwagon, or ride the crest of this wave [6 months too late]. Last year there were a lot of buyers in the market because for 6 years Property had been going up and up and up and there were TV shows and radio shows and everything in the papers about Property. Get into Property because Property prices are growing and they'll never stop growing now quick. Be quick.

Now they've all gone back underground. That is the fundamental difference between 2001-2007, and what we're experiencing right now in 2008.

Summary

In the times of a downturn, when most buyers are scared, you can take advantage and make cash. A buyers market is defined by a lack of buyers, giving the few buyers out there control of price due to a lack of competition. People will always need to sell, so the buyers still in the market have control and negotiation power.

Forget growth [for now], think yield

Like Groundhog Day year on year on year, every 7-10 years, every 7-10 years, every 7-10 years, Property values will double.

Since 2001 there's been a lot of growth in the market and people have succeeded in [made cash] getting equity growth in their portfolio. Many 'accidental' investors made money and a lot of people have seen their portfolio double in 3, 5 or 7 years; which is fantastic.

Things are very different now.

To buy Property 18-30% below market value *right now* and to make cash in Property *right now,* you need to forget about growth. Really. For now, just forget it.

At the moment it's not about growth; we may not experience any growth, we might get negative growth. We might go down 20% in the next 6 months [we certainly aren't going to pretend to have a crystal ball]. Who knows, none of us know. We can all predict [guess] but none of us know for sure.

We've just stopped thinking about it. It doesn't matter. We'll never have timing exactly worked out; otherwise we'd be billionaires this time next year, Rodney.

Making Property investment decisions now based on growth in our opinion isn't the right strategy for making cash, and it's not the right short term strategy; it's your long term view.

When we say forget about growth, we don't care if the Property market goes down 50% tomorrow. We don't care if every single one of our properties is worth £1 next month. Really. It's not likely, but it doesn't matter.

We know that shocks, surprises [and scares] a lot of people but we really aren't focused on growth because we're not thinking short term about growth, we're thinking long term about growth. We know that in the long term even if everyone of our properties goes down to £1 each in 10 years time [never going to happen] they will have gone back up to £200,000 [if they were worth £100,000], somewhere in keeping with historical values.

We never know when the peaks and troughs are going to be, but we know that we have the long term strategy sorted. Done and dusted. Buy with as little cash as possible [zero risk, infinite ROI] and hold forever.

For the short term, how do we cover all the bases and how do you negate the negative impact of any negative growth? Wasn't that poetic! Good and important question too. There's only one way.

The mistake that most people make is this: they buy properties based on their [so called] discounts, and they expect [or bank on] growth to make money. For example: properties double every 7-10 years so they think: 'In 2 years my Property will have gone up 20%, in 4 years 40%, in 6 years 60% [and so on].'

They pin all their hopes and expectations on that cash coming incrementally, and that's where they fail because growth does not come incrementally.

They forget the Law of compounding, don't they [from our last book]?!

You can't rely on growth exactly and incrementally, you have to take it as an average over the long term. Your growth curve may not be as smooth in the next 3 years as it has been over the last 30.

In 10 years it will have doubled, but in 2 years it might not have moved at all [a very real possibility right now]. You can't expect growth to deliver you cashflow steadily and incrementally just when you want it. It's not your bitch. It comes when it comes and you have to take it when it comes, and build it in your strategy.

What we're looking for is **yield**. Now you know the general definition of yield because we've got it in our last book. For buying Property right now [very cheaply] you need to make sure that the yield of your Property is high enough, and we would suggest you should be finding 7%-9% [gross].

The last 2 deals we have done have been 7.8% yield [£550 rent on a purchase price of £70,000] and 7.5% [£450 rent on a purchase price of £60,000].

Last year 6% yield was good for us. This year it is unacceptable.

Sometimes, in today's market, you can get 10, 11 even 12%+ gross yield. Beware: many end up being 4% net yield because of all of the costs. For single let Property you should be looking to achieve about 7-9% yield now, much better than 9 months before, because rents are going up and you can buy your properties much cheaper.

If you buy Property with a good yield and your mortgage is more than covered by your rent [plus all of the additional running costs of that portfolio], your Property will cashflow. Whether it's cashflowing £1, £10 £50 or £100 [per month]; it's cashflowing. By definition you have an asset.

It doesn't matter if the actual value of that asset is zero because it still produces income; it still produces cash. It's like in the stock market: it doesn't really matter what the value of a stock is, if it's producing a dividend, it's an asset.

This is fundamentally important. If you buy a Property which is negatively cashflowing **and** it's dropping in value then you're losing money on a monthly basis 2 ways. That's 2 big holes in the bottom of your money box. At any one time you could have an asset that's not worth what you paid for it [not worth what you want it to be worth], and you've compounded your troubles by losing money out of your other income streams every month.

You need to [by definition] be buying assets. *An asset is something that produces income*. You can't rely on growth for income *in the current market* so you have to rely on cashflow.

Summary

We're not expecting too much growth for the short term, so forget it for now; it will happen later. Look for big discounts, high rents and good cashflow. You can realistically achieve yields of 8% on single let Property if you buy well in today's market.

Why now is the best time to buy [for 10 years?]

You won't find this in many other Property books. This is one of the sections where we're not talking about concepts or long term strategies [which are very important]. This section is time sensitive, applicable right now, and your ability to succeed will depend on how quickly you grasp this and how quickly you *put into action* what you read.

The Property market goes through cycles just like anything else; life, birth, youth, adolescence, middle age, old age, death; everything goes through cycles. Anyone who has studied economics or anyone who understands life in general knows that we go through these 'seasons.'

Understanding this is going to help you succeed in the Property market, especially right now. Most people just believe that the Property market will always, always, always go up every single year after year after year.

Most of those are now bankrupt.

The Property market will go round in cycles; the growth curve of the market will go through troughs as well as peaks.

We liken the market to seasons. At any given period of time you might experience a 'hot market' [summer] a 'cool market' [autumn] a 'warm market' [spring] and a cold market [winter]. We're going to explain these seasons in detail and show you what period of the market we're in, when the best time to buy is and when the best time to wait, hold or slow your buying is, if that's OK with you now.

This knowledge will definitely put you in the top 1%, we are convinced of that. This section is taken from how a professional, serious Property investor would view the market: an investor who **makes cash regularly**, fast and perpetually.

If we read the papers, act like the Sheep and Crabs, watch the TV and listen to the radio, we would be fooled into viewing the market from the wrong way around, inside out and back to front. We would believe that a 'hot market' is one where the Property prices are going up and a cold market is one where the Property prices are going down.

Don't forget that the 'speculative' or novice investors, first time buyers or owner-occupiers are **always too late**. They're usually at least 6 months or a year too late; a season too late. By the time they get into the market and their perception is that it's a growing [or falling] market, and by the time they manage to convince themselves and follow all the other Sheep, they're going in the wrong direction.

Once you really get this you'll make money.

Summer

A summer Property market is a buyers' market; there are far more sellers than buyers. You will usually get some kind of 'credit crunch' or 'mortgage crisis' [like we have right now] and maybe you'll experience a hike in interest rates. The cost of living could go up, unemployment could rise, inflation could be at a higher level, or you could get a combination of many or all of these happening at once.

This causes people to have less disposable income. Loans that people have on their properties and additional loans they've taken out become harder and harder to repay because they have less spare cash. They default on their unsecured debt first [credit cards, store cards, hire purchase etc] and when things get even worse, as they probably will through the rest of 2008/9, they default on their secured loans [mortgages, larger loans and consolidation loans].

They are in serious debt and they need to sell very quickly to stop repossession and get their hands on some money from their properties to get out of the hole that they are in. Most people don't understand the buy and hold strategy; they just understand buying and selling.

At the apex of the hot summer market the buyers have control. If a seller needs to sell, and there will always be sellers who need to sell, there are far less buyers who are not competing with each other. They can **control the price.**

The properties are cheap and the yields are high.

In this summer market you want to be buying as many as you can, as fast as you can, as often as you can and as cheaply as you can, and you want to keep going and going and going. This is what the professional investor will be doing.

You want to be in on it at this stage, you want to be hot; that's why you've bought this book.

You want to be on every estate agent's mailing list. You want every Property finder to have your details. You want to be viewing as many properties as possible. You want to be offering on everything you view. You want to be offering on everything at 30-35% below market value. You want to help estate agents out. You want to go and view as many properties as you can [even if you didn't originally intend to buy them]. You want to be leaflet dropping over and over in the areas where yield is highest. The more of these that you can do, the more you can **get mindspace awareness** and the more likely you'll be to find those motivated sellers.

Important point: the market isn't always going to be like this. It's not always going to be this simple [not easy] to buy Property. It's not always going to be this cheap. The general public are not always going to have such low sentiment.

This is the time when you can fill your boots. If you just bought 5 properties this year at 30% below market value [achievable with clear rules], all at around £100,000, you'd instantly make £150,000 in discount [equity] buying under market value. You could cashflow those properties at let's say £50-£100 a month each [net after all of you costs], therefore making £250-£500 a month cashflow.

For more detailed figures, go to page 389.

Once we come out of this hot summer market [for the serious investor] and go into a cooler spring or autumn market, the Property prices will start to rise again and you will start to get capital growth. You will make money 3 ways. You could potentially make £150,000 just for buying the properties, £250-£500 per month cashflow, and then £50,000 compounding growth a year for the next 10, 20, 50 years. All off the back of one hot summer Property market that may last a year or 2.

It's not very often that you will experience a summer buying market. You'll remember from earlier in the book that the statistics indicate that it will be one year in every 10 as an average, so these chances may be few and far between. We may be 40 before it happens again!

Since 1952, according to Nationwide, the following years have experienced a downturn in the Property market. We have put the figures for all types of Property for the whole country here as a percentage this time:

1953: -1%
1954: -1%
1990: -10.7%
1991: -2.3%
1992: -6.5%
1995: -2.3%

That's 6 years out of 58.

Autumn

Then other professional investors begin to latch on to this as they become a little bit more aware, and then they start bidding with each other.

At the moment we're one of only 2 or 3 investors in the market in Peterborough but within 6-12 months there'll be other investors who'll cotton on to this, who've finally found a way to get finance, and all of a sudden we'll be competing with more people. Therefore it won't be quite as easy to get the 18-30% below market value deals.

When investors start bidding against each other and forcing the sale prices up slightly, the vendors start increasing their selling price because they know they can achieve that higher sale price [because there are more buyers in the market].

Then the professional investors start offering even more for the properties because there's more competition. The vendors have put their prices up. Because of this owner-occupiers and first time buyers struggle to get on to the residential housing market. The lending criteria for buy to let mortgages are less strict than they are for residential or personal mortgages, so that compounds their challenge of getting on the housing market.

This pushes price up even further.

You get speculative investors who come into the market [later than the professionals] who start bidding against the professional investors and owner-occupiers. As they outbid the professional investor Property Ladder, Homes Under the Hammer style, prices are pushed up even further.

The professional investor gets pushed out of the market. They can't buy the properties cheaply enough for the deals to work for them according to their rules and personal deal analysers. The professional investor will bide his time and knows that there's only a certain amount of money they can pay for Property to make them work from a cashflow perspective.

They have experience and they know what's happening. **They do not get emotional about it.**

The speculative investor has still got to learn these lessons. Because they've come into the market without this knowledge, they start buying higher spec properties because that's their personal preference [emotion].

Many of us, when we first get into Property investment, don't realise that we want to buy the cheap, ugly properties; we don't realise that they're the money boxes. Many people baulk when they see the properties we buy.

'Oh, er, ah, um, OK. That wasn't quite what I was expecting'

Then there's a long blank and slightly embarrassed gaze.

You certainly wouldn't see them on Property ladder!

Inexperienced investors assume that the better looking properties that they would rather live in, that would attract a higher rent [lower yield], would be a better investment.

The owner-occupiers and first time buyers still need to buy and they still need to places to live. There will always be first time buyers and owner-occupiers who need to buy. The owner-occupiers in the market adapt and you start to see smaller properties with smaller footprints. You get multiple occupiers and couples getting a mortgage together making their lending criteria slightly easier. You get shared ownership where up to 5 people can own one house and each individual can borrow less but afford more.

So they start to kick back, and they start to then outbid the speculative investors. While all of this is happening the market value is being pushed up.

The owner-occupiers are back in the market because they've adapted and the market's adapted. They've pushed the speculative investors up so far where even they have cottoned on to the fact that they can no longer afford to buy these properties.

The speculative investors' properties [new, off-plan] will start to show themselves in their true light. They'll start to complete on their properties and the figures will show that they're making a loss because of their miscalculations and lack of experience. They let their emotions get involved and they got into bidding wars. They started outbidding the professional investors and owner-occupiers.

They start to panic [Sheep and Crabs] and they start to sell their properties back to owner-occupiers. They try to release some kind of capital gain. Very often this can actually end up being a loss because they were new to the game, didn't have enough experience, got pulled in to the crest of a marketing wave, their rental calculations were optimistic, or the discount they achieved wasn't what they thought it was.

When you come towards the end of the autumn period [the cooling spot], the owner-occupiers are then left with unsuitable properties or high mortgages because the whole process of events has pushed prices up. Owner-occupiers have paid premium prices for properties because of speculative or novice investors, and now they're left over-geared.

This is exactly what has happened over the last 2-3 years with lending; banks being far too willing to lend and being far too lenient with their entrance criteria.

Speculative investors and owner-occupiers have been able to borrow and over-extend themselves and they've got to a point now where they're either in negative equity, their Property portfolios are shortfalling considerably, or they've got a mortgage that they just can't afford to pay.

Winter

With the recent mortgage crisis, the credit crunch, the increase in oil, food and electricity and the cost of living, people can no longer afford these high mortgages [which they probably couldn't afford to buy in the first place]. Maybe, when things looked rosy, they bought a 4 bed when they could really only afford a 3 bed, or a 3 bed instead of a 2 bed [because they could get away with it]. The banks made it easier for them to borrow the extra money.

The speculative investor has sold [very often at a loss]. As this happens repossession rates start to rise because many of the speculative investors get caught with their pants down. The same thing happens to owner-occupiers who have over-borrowed.

Some areas start reporting negative equity, many investors have geared almost to 100%, and once the prices begin to drop, banks start restricting and pulling back on their lending. They start making it much more difficult to borrow money; they increase their interest rates or they make you jump through many more hoops to get finance. This phases out many owner-occupiers, first time buyers and also many speculative investors.

The lenders will start to suffer. As they lend less and less money they make less and less money. Lenders want to lend because they want to make money! The only way lenders make money is to lend money!

The speculative investors are selling and realising a loss, many owner-occupiers are defaulting on unsecured lending just to try and meet their mortgage payments, therefore getting into more and more debt. There comes a point where many mortgage companies [banks] lose money on missed mortgage payments and the cost of repossessing and recovering bad debt.

Throughout this winter period, it's not always the best time to buy. The reason for that is that you are going to have to shortfall your properties [pay for your properties out of your own pocket]. It's not until we leave this cold period and hit back into the spring and summer that you can actually make any good money buying Property.

You want to be spending as little as you can and saving as much money as you can at this time. This may not be the best time for you to buy in your area, and you may have to be more selective. Save all the money that you would have used to invest because when the next summer or spring market arises, these are the times that you want to buy in abundance.

We personally like to keep buying through all the seasons. Your choice will be down to you, your rules and your vision. Our buying and negotiation power, our marketing, our relationships with agents and our goals all allow us to continue to buy perpetually. We just have to keep adjusting our strategy.

When you know that you can consistently get deals, that you need to keep your channels of leads open, and you want to keep from getting rusty, you'll keep buying too, because you can.

Don't go getting excessive finance, don't go buying fantasy Cars and don't go on fancy holidays. Save as much money as you can. The more liquid you are in the spring and summer seasons, the more you'll be able to make hay, so be aware of your spending in times like these.

Spring

Areas can then start to become flooded with properties and supply outweighs demand. Look at city centres like Nottingham and Manchester recently, they became flooded with properties, especially new flats, over recent years. Many buyers experienced poor cash flow through decreased rents, lost money through falling prices and developers experienced the same fate. Once developers pull out of developments and stop building you know things are potentially good for you, the professional investor.

The professional investor's eyes will start to open again. She will realise that yields will start to turn favourable at last. She will be able to begin to buy very cheap properties like she was doing in the hot summer market. Through the cool and the cold markets she may not be interested in buying because she might not be able to buy cheaply enough. But now that the supply is exceeding demand there will be many of these properties that will have to be sold very cheaply.

The professional investors can start to bid lower on the middle to higher end of the market. Many of these newer developments and slightly more exclusive areas are no longer exclusive because too many have been built. They can start to really bid the prices down making them attractive investment propositions again. They can start getting the yields on these properties by buying them with large discounts. They become less interested in the lower end of the market and consequently it forces the lower end of the market down.

Generally speaking, it's the lower end of the market which produces the greater yields, so from a professional investor's point of view this is a good thing to happen. Of course at the same time the first time buyers or the owner-occupiers are still not willing to come back into the market because they're still bruised; behind the times by 6-12 months. This forces the prices of properties down because they're not in the market either.

Therefore opportunity arises again between the spring and summer buying market. The few Property investors who are liquid, who've saved money through the autumn and winter buying markets, who can get finance, who are open to the opportunities and are ready now, can start to buy many considerably under value properties at the lower end of the market.

The full cycle

So we've taken a full cycle in the Property market but where does that leave us right now? Well you've probably already guessed where that leaves us right now, haven't you?

Yes it does depend a little on your area, but currently the market we are in is somewhere between spring and summer from a buyer's perspective. By the time you read this book, that may or may not have changed, but it doesn't matter because you know the difference, don't you?

These concepts do change from area to area and are presented generically. Currently in our area in Peterborough we're very much in a summer period. This may not last forever and will need to continually look at our strategy. If Peterborough does become a winter or an autumn buying market then we'll have to look at buying in other areas if we want to maintain the current volume and buying price.

If this is the case then we'll trailblaze an area in which we can set up shop and localise there to catch it in a spring or summer market.

Because Property is not liquid, because Property is not like putting your card into the cash machine at the bank, it very much plays into the professional Property investor's hands. When people really need to sell Property they can't just go to the cashpoint and get their money out. When people want to buy, it can be 3-6 months before the transaction is complete. That can cost an owner-occupier or an investor dearly, especially an investor who's looking to use the buy, remortgage, refurb, remortgage strategy.

You can place yourself at a huge advantage by being liquid and having access to finance or cash. If you don't yet, don't worry, it won't stop you. But remember it for the next summer market; you'll be very glad you did!

Summary

The Property market goes around in cycles, just like everything else. Understanding the cycle will enable you to take advantage and plan your strategy years in advance. Most people see the Property cycle the wrong way around: you can make hay while other people are in a state of fear and panic.

Section 4: Psychology

Psychology is quite possibly the most important part of any investment strategy. If you desire money, success, happiness and free time, you will need the mindset to make it happen.

Most people overlook the importance of psychology because what most people are after are the 3 or 7 or 10 secrets; the tools, the tricks, the strategies, the hidden formulas, the golden rules that make something work; that makes investing and making money easy.

They are so busy looking for the details that they miss the details; they miss the things that are really important, as covered in this section.

Making money and making Property a success is simple but it's not easy. Success is simple in that you can look at all of the psychological Laws of success and the psychology of successful people; commitment, action, desire, focus, faith and so on [as stated in "The 44 Most Closely Guarded Property Secrets"] and you can replicate them [benchmarking].

That's pretty simple.

People love to over complicate things but the fact remains that copying a step by step process, even a psychological one, is pretty simple; like a set of instructions, a blueprint or a map.

But of course most people don't end up doing it, so it's not as easy as one would expect. If it were easy, everybody would be doing it, wouldn't they?!

Well actually, no. Otherwise it would change the rules. There would be no 80/20.

However, if you are looking for specific strategies then the next 7 psychological Laws will make you successful in Property, especially in the times of a Property market crash [downturn]. Follow them. Use them. Make them part of who you are.

In our first book, "The 44 Most Closely Guarded Property Secrets" you had an overall view of the psychology of successful Property investors, wealthy business owners and successful people. In this book we take that to another level and give you the psychological Laws of success for people making money in this market, because it takes a certain kind of person to make money in this market.

You know that there are more millionaires made in a 'recession' than at any other time. However, the opportunities that are out there at the moment aren't being utilised by many people because they don't have one, some or all of the following simple traits:

Opportunism

Being open, awake and aware of what's going on; seeing and taking your chance when it comes. That's opportunism.

A lot of people, [Sheep and Crabs] live with their heads in the sand praying that the 'problem' will go away, but of course that just compounds the problem, doesn't it? Not opening your bills doesn't make your bills go away; they go from white to red and in the end you get beaten up or put in prison by men who look like they've come straight out of Reservoir Dogs.

The people who really do make money in a Property market crash are the people who are looking for the opportunities. Seek and Ye shall find, an important person once said.

Rather than being down, depressed, staying up all night with worry about the market, or just doing nothing because 'there's no money to be made in the Property market,' *be aware of what's happening*. Be realistic about what's happening, but at the same time look for the opportunities that are out there every hour of every day.

You will find those opportunities because as you know, you get what you focus on. Being opportunistic isn't very difficult. Because things change so much in the market we are in right now, opportunities can come out of nowhere.

We've been seeing mortgage rates go up and up and up like we've never seen before, and by the same level they can come down. A deal that looked like it worked 2 weeks ago may have totally changed. Sometimes when finance is very difficult to find, the people who are opportunistic and actively looking for the answers will find answers. Very often those answers will be better than the answers they had before.

The fact that finance is so hard to find right now has opened a great opportunity to buy Property cheaper than ever before.

2 great examples of opportunism in the modern world that we particularly like are that of the conception of Facebook and the Post It note.

Facebook was never initially 'designed' to be a worldwide social networking phenomenon. When Facebook was first started by Mark Zuckerberg in his Harvard dorm, it was purely for him and his friends to better connect with other schoolmates.

Had Mark Zuckerberg not seen an opportunity in Web 2.0 and the power of social networking [before many others], and the many venture capitalists that backed him, it would still be confined to Harvard University. It is now a worldwide addiction, generating billions of dollars in ad revenue, and changing the way that both marketing and networking is done online.

The second story of opportunism that inspires us is the Post It note. The Post It note is possibly one of the most widely used inventions of our time [and the most simple]. Ironically enough 3M, the company behind the Post It notes, weren't looking for Post It notes to be Post it notes!

They were trying to find a glue that would stick well; a strong adhesive. Spence Silver was working on the project and was not successful. He was making mistakes and finding that when they were testing the glue it was very weak and wouldn`t hold on to anything.

Silver decided not to reject the glue just yet.

4 years later, 3M scientist Arthur Fry was singing in his Church choir using paper markers to remember pages, but they kept falling out.
Remembering Silver's glue, he used it on the paper markers and found it strong enough to stick but weak enough to peel off without damaging the pages.

There we have it, the birth of the Post It note.

There are hundreds of stories every day about people who built huge businesses that hinged on moments of opportunism.

Oh, go on then, one last story of opportunity. 2 young guys who are members of one of the largest internet marketing groups in the world were looking to make money online.

They set up a business clearing dog turd [yes you read it right!] from people's gardens, advertising online. A somewhat strange online business it would seem, but there are all sorts of crazy niches you would not believe.

Side note: a good friend and business partner of ours makes over £10,000 per year on his eCommerce site selling Bumble Bee outfits. That's one niche product out of 100's he sells.

Another friend made £35,000 per year for 2 years selling adult nappies on eBay to people in Japan!

So clearing dog shit online doesn't seem quite so niche now, does it?! And they became pretty successful at this clearing business. So successful that their parents sat them down and asked them what they were going to do about the massive and ever growing pile of dog turd that was taking over their garden.

Now they have a problem.

Being entrepreneurial is all about solving problems. Where they got this idea, we'll never know, but it's pretty irrelevant.

The 2 young entrepreneurs set up a new sister business that would sell, box and send a gift wrapped dog turd to any address of your choice.

'If there's someone you don't like, we can gift wrap a dog turd and send it to them for you, anywhere in the world!'

This business became successful very quickly. Their stockpile of dog turd was being used faster than they could clear it using their first business, and a new problem soon faced them: no stock!

They had sold all of the dog shit and had to dramatically upscale!

A true story!

Summary

Fall asleep in this market and you'll miss all the fun and money. You have to take your chance when it comes, because we are in a wormhole of opportunity and we don't know how long it is going to last. Be inspired by the many great stories of opportunism.

Flexibility

The second psychological Law of success in a Property market downturn.

As we've stated many times in our books, markets can change very very quickly. Don't blink. There have been 6 or 7 years of boom; out-performing market growth. The companies, investors and businesses that have spent all of their time focusing on the same strategy [new build, off plan, overseas, daylight bridging, vendor paid deposits] are now finding it tough and face losing a lot of money. In this fast changing world, you need to be able to adapt like lightning.

We personally know an investor who had 86 properties in his portfolio. Funnily enough he bought them all pretty well, at a good discount and in an efficient way. However he made some fundamental errors. He was gearing them up too high [sometimes to 100%], spending cash-backs and buying properties all over the country.

There are many reasons why he went bankrupt and lost his portfolio. One of the major ones was that when the criteria changed for mortgage lending, he wasn't flexible, he couldn`t move quickly enough and the rate increases caused him problems.

Life is transient and things change so much faster now than they used to. People get new jobs every year, and the internet is moving technology faster and faster ahead. You need to keep on top of what is happening out there.

That's being able to have more than one broker that you put your deals through, being able to strike up win-win deals with vendors and being creative about finance so you can buy a Property at 30% below market value. It's going on viewings immediately when people ask, and taking time out of your day so that you're the first investor on the scene to make the offer, to get the deal and to build the best relationships.

Things are not the same as they were last year, 3 years ago or 5 years before that. 10 or 20 years ago and we're almost back in the Stone Age with the speed at which things change now. Most people didn't have a mobile and Facebook didn't exist. It's a little scary, but it is the land of unparalleled opportunity if you're open and creative.

Summary

The market is changing so fast; deals and finance keep changing every week. In order to stay ahead, buy cheap Property and attain finance, you have to be flexible and creative. Life is in constant change. Embrace it, go with it and cash in on it.

Contrarianism

The third psychological law of success in times of a Property market downturn.

This is something that is very specific to the times we're in right now. Quite possibly the most famous investor to make money in what you might call a 'downturn,' someone you would call a 'contrarian investor,' someone who is doing the opposite to everyone else is George Soros. He's made billions of dollars on the stock market buying when everyone else was selling, and selling when everyone else was buying.

'He believed that financial markets can best be described as chaotic. The prices of securities and currencies depend on human beings, or the traders - both professional and non-professional - who buy and sell these assets. These persons often act out based on emotion, rather than logical considerations.

He also believed that market participants influenced one another and moved in herds. He always watched for an opportunity to get out in front and "make a killing." How could he tell when the time was right? Soros has said that he would have an instinctive physical reaction about when to buy and sell, making his strategy a difficult model to emulate.'

This was taken directly from Wikipedia. George Soros was famous for making $2Billion in one day [risking $10Billion] and was coined as 'the man who broke the Bank of England.'

Being a contrarian investor takes a certain kind of personality, which of course can [and should] be learned. At the moment we are right in the heart of a buyers' market. Most buyers are no longer buying. The first time buyers can't get on the ladder. Novice and 'speculative' investors are finding it hard because they don't know enough. Even experienced or 'professional' investors who haven't experienced a downturn before are not buying any more. They don't have some of the psychological strengths that they need in this market yet.

So while the Sheep are all going that way, while all the Rats are running out of town in the same direction, the people who are making the real money are the people who are doing the opposite.

The definition of that is 'Contrarian' investment.

So to give you the example relevant to the Property market right now, currently at the time of writing this book the competition that we have in our Property market in Peterborough buying has gone down from around 12 investors down to just 2 other people.

In Peterborough it has been reported that there are now 15 properties to one buyer. That's a pretty amazing statistic.

We're no longer in the Property business; we are in the fruit business. Specifically we are in the Cherry picking business right now!

Can you not see the opportunity in this? The opportunity to buy at such a reduced rate because we're *doing the opposite of what everyone else is doing.*

There will always be people who need to sell. In this time of a market downturn, it's not just the Property market, it's the potential of a whole recession, and the 'credit crunch.' A lot of people are geared far too high, they're in debt; they're at 100 – 120% of income versus expenditure.

If people are in debt and they're about to be repossessed, then they have no choice but to sell at a price which somebody can buy very quickly, or be repossessed. And who wants the pain and embarrassment of being repossessed?

People don't all of a sudden stop getting divorced in the time of a Property market downturn, people don't stop having babies, people don't stop having families, people don't stop dying, and people don't stop moving, relocating and emigrating.

Life goes on and when people need to sell, they need to sell. If they need to sell right now and they're motivated, and if you're one of the 2 or 3 buyers in your area, you will make hay [cash], no doubt about it.

This scenario enables you to control price because no one else is going to come and bid higher. You are a contrarian investor doing the opposite to everyone else. That's why you dramatically increase your chances right now of buying 30% below market value. In a rising market, [when competing with 12-15 other speculative, professional investors and owner-occupiers] if you go and put offers in [as many as you can] at 30-35% plus below market value, you will always get beaten. You'll have very little hope of hitting the bullseye with many of those offers.

But right now you can control the price at which you buy. You have negotiation power [more later]. Once the sellers have the control again, you will not be able to buy anywhere near as cheaply as you can now. No one knows when that might be, but if you sit there scratching yourself then you might miss all the fun.

Most people will see a Property market boom as a great thing, which it is if you hold a big portfolio and it's growing. But it's not the best time to buy.

It's the 80/20 or the 99/1 principle. It's simple vs. easy. This is simple: *do what everyone else isn't doing*. But it's not easy because sometimes, like when all the Rats are running out of town, it's quite difficult to walk the opposite way. You might be walking into a flood, a fire, an earthquake or a nuclear explosion. But it's the people who have the strength and the belief, who've done the diligence and the research, who trust themselves with conviction, faith and confidence, who are making all of the money.

Summary

More millionaires are made in a recession than at any other time. They don't make all this money doing what everyone else is doing; they make it when the majority of people are in a state of panic and fear. People will sell their properties well below market value when the market is going down and sentiment is low.

Decision

This is the fourth psychological trait of successful Property investors.

This was actually included in "The 44 Most Closely Guarded Property Secrets" and we wanted to add to it in this book because it's very important. When we talk about decision we are looking at *speed of decision* in this particular instance, at this particular time.

When things are changing so quickly you need to *act fast*. Yes you need to do your diligence, you need to do your research, you need to know your market, you need to know your Property type, you need to know your yield, you need to know what to buy and what not to buy, and that's great. Most people get stuck in the details.

They get stuck in analysis paralysis. Rabbit in the headlights.

Act and act fast. If you get a phone call from a distressed seller you get over to that house right now because if you don't the other buyer[s] in the market will. If you're doing assignable contracts or bridging loans and if the mortgage products are changing every 2 weeks, then your ability to get your mortgage or remortgage will depend on your speed. Investor friends of ours believe that many financial products only have a 6 week shelf life in todays market.

People will not make money in their sleep in this market downturn.

Don't hang around waiting for the paint to dry.

And that's all we need to say. A quick and decisive chapter!

Summary

Be diligent and well informed; then act fast. Make decisions quickly and stick by them. Procrastination is a disease of the sofa.

Faith & trust [in yourself]

The fifth psychological trait of successful property investors in a Property market downturn is faith and trust.

'Self-trust is the first secret of success,' according to Ralph Waldo Emerson.

We've put these 2 together because they're essentially the same thing. When all the Rats are running out of town and all the Sheep are grazing on that piece of grass over there, [which is bare and empty because they're all there on the same spot eating it], it's sometimes difficult to have that continued *faith* in yourself. If you haven't seen the results of what you're looking for [yet] that can make it even tougher, especially if the market could go down even further.

Anything you ever achieve in your life is because you've had some kind of *faith in yourself and you trusted yourself* that you could and would achieve it; you had faith in your instinct and intuition.

You may be the only person who has faith in your ability to buy at 30% below market value. You may be the only person who believes that these properties can be bought in the market right now. You may be the only person who believes that there are creative ways to buy these deals. No one else is going to do it for you.

Think now of anything that you have achieved in your life.

We mean right now, so go for it. Take a break for a minute and think about one thing, anything, no matter how big or small, that you have achieved in your life. Perhaps you bought something you thought you could never afford. Perhaps you helped someone achieve something they were proud of. Perhaps, [like Rob] you're punching above your weight and you have a girlfriend [or boyfriend] who is far too good looking for you!

Our guess is that you didn't always have it; the ownership or the sense of achievement. In order to get to that place; to have that feeling, you must have believed that you could. You must have had faith in yourself to do it, get it, have it and go for it.

It is impossible not to. Get it, I mean. Do it now. You can't not.

Not if you have faith and trust in yourself now.

We personally love inspirational stories. One of the most inspirational stories is that of Victor Frankl, who wrote 'Man's search for meaning.'

If you haven't read the book yet, we recommend that you read it once you have finished this one. It will make your 'problems' seem very insignificant.

The story is about Victor Frankl's life in Nazi death camps and its lessons for spiritual survival. Here is the publisher's synopsis:

'Between 1942 and 1945 psychiatrist Viktor Frankl labored in 4 different camps, including Auschwitz, while his parents, brother, and pregnant wife perished. Based on his own experience and the stories of his many patients, Frankl argues that we cannot avoid suffering but we can choose how to cope with it, find meaning in it, and move forward with renewed purpose. Frankl's theory—known as logotherapy, from the Greek word logos ["meaning"]—holds that our primary drive in life is not pleasure, as Freud maintained, but the discovery and pursuit of what we personally find meaningful. "What man actually needs," Frankl writes, "is not a tensionless state but rather the striving and struggling for a worthwhile goal, a freely chosen task . . . the call of a potential meaning waiting to be fulfilled by him."

It was faith that kept Victor alive when all around him were killed.

We are also inspired by Lance Armstrong and the Livestrong foundation that he set up. We could not even do the stories justice, so you can read them on the Livestrong website: livestrong.org

Livestrong is our designated charity that we donate some of the proceeds of this book to. Please take time to read the site, you'll be very inspired.

Summary

Believe in yourself and your abilities. Have faith in yourself and trust yourself to make the right decisions most of the time [and you will].

Timing

In the current market timing is very important, but not in the way that most people think.

We have spoken to hundreds and thousands of people at all different levels of Property investing from zero to 500 properties. Never once have we ever met anybody in all of our experience who is able to tell us *accurately, exactly, time and time again* when the market will be at its lowest or highest, when it will bottom out, when it will peak, when it will boom and when it will crash. Never.

The fundamental mistake that most people make over and over is that they are trying to time and second guess the market; they believe they can predict when it will be at its lowest and it's highest. This is a huge mistake that most investors make in the stock market too. You cannot predict exactly when a stock may go down or up. You can predict that it can, or will, but not when.

It is time intensive and energy draining.

It's the same in the Property market. I've [Mark] spoken to people who have said 'oh the market's gonna crash,' and they were telling me this in 2001. Some were telling me this in 1995:

'I'm not investing, I'm going to wait until the Property market has crashed and bottomed out and it goes back up.'

Of course those people have waited years and years and if they'd bought just 5 properties in 1995, those properties would have tripled in value.

That's a bloody expensive waiting game that they're playing, waiting for the market to 'bottom out.'

Understanding that you can never time the market exactly stops you wasting your life trying and failing every time. It may be a belief and I may miss one chance in 10, but to me trying to time the market is gambling, not investing.

For the sake of myself, Rob, our team at Progressive and our investors making money, a belief that serves us all much better is that I can't predict when the market is going to be at its lowest or highest. I just have to be aware of what's going on and be decisive, flexible and be opportunistic.

At the moment, who knows when the market will stop going down? So many people are talking about a 10, 20, even 30% drop; but how can they actually tell? They're all playing the same crystal ball game. The current perception of the market is definitely warped; there's a lot of wayward sentiment and propaganda flying around and you have to cut through all that and find the *reality* for you.

When I speak to good friends and contacts in financial markets in the city they believe that it could be another 18 months before this 'crisis' is over. The huge slowdown in Property transactions is now 'official' and worse than that of the late 80's.

The Bank of England now predicts that it could last a long while and have taken a tougher stance, having initially tried to cover up the full extent of the whole 'credit crunch.'

The point is that sentiment changes all the time, even from the experts.

What we do know is that there is opportunity to buy Property much cheaper than last year, and that might continue through to next year and beyond [who knows].

Let me make this clear: you can only ever buy Property **right now, in the moment.** You can't buy Property last year. Yes you can wait until next year, but who knows what's going to happen next year. So the age old cliché comes out again: you don't wait to buy Property, you buy Property and wait. You **buy as well as you can now** and you use current market factors to your advantage.

Time waits for nobody.

Now is a great time to buy. You've probably heard us say this 15 times already in this book and we'll just keep drumming it into you. By the time you've read this book, you will know that now is a great time to buy. If it takes 7 times to convince the 'average' person then there should be no reason left in the world why you're not convinced by the end of the book.

I personally believe [Rob] we're in a vacuum at the moment where there's great opportunity because of the lack of lending and the illiquid market. In our direct experience this has created a false drop in the market and has created a unique situation. If you even want to get a Property through [borrow money on it at a reasonable rate] you have to buy really cheap Property.

Dirty cheap as Simon and Mark like to call it. I keep trying to get them to use another word for it, but we know what they mean.

To give you some evidence, here are some basic figures of the last 2 deals that we have bought:

Property type: 2 bed flat
Location: Fletton
Purchase price: £70,000
Refurb cost: £6,000
Market value/revaluation: £105,000
Rent: £550
Percentage discount: 33%

Property type: 1 bed flat
Location: Peterborough city
Asking price: £89,995
Purchase price: £60,000
Refurb cost: £1,500
Market value/revaluation: £85,000
Rent: £450
Percentage discount: 30%

In 6, 12 or 18 months time, or whenever the credit crunch is all over, everyone's happy again and the banks are lending and the market is going back up, you won't have that pressure on the vendors and on people who can't buy because they can't raise finance.

Calm will resume. Confidence will resume. People will become carefree [careless] again and you won't have anywhere near the negotiation power anymore; your vendors won't be in a situation where they have no other choice. They'll pull that power right back and demand more money for their Property.

And if we're down another 10, 15 or 20% in one year then the people who said 'I'm not going to invest now, I'm going to follow the flock and I'm going to wait and I told you it would go down another 10% blah blah blah...'

...Well they've actually missed an opportunity to buy even cheaper than when they come back into the market at their predicted bottom out point [if they ever do]. The mortgage crisis and the increased cost of living [which haven't happened anything like this for years] have probably added 10-15% to the discount you had been getting in the 'crash.'

That's not always going to happen. That's not happened in the last 10 years, it may not happen ever again. Yes the market may go down another 10% but if lending is more liquid [as it is likely to be] then you might still be buying at the same price then as you were 6 months before, or you may even be buying at a higher price! You have to take the whole picture into account here.

We are currently buying at prices that people expect the market to be in 12-18 months. They don't know it, but they are pre-empting the crash before the market actually goes down in reality.

Sentiment and Expectation theory.

How can we be sure of that? Because there is no way that the market has dropped 25-33% in the last 9 months. We know the statistics: asking prices are still up, surveyors are still valuing properties at no less than 5% less than they were 9 months ago, and sales are still going through Rightmove and the agents at levels that we can still undercut by 25%.

Summary

Timing in this market is everything. Most people are waiting for it all to end like some kind of storm. *Act fast* and you will buy Property as cheap as you ever have; perhaps the cheapest you will for another 10-20 years.

Relationships

Way back in the early 1900's Napoleon Hill wrote 'Think and Grow Rich.' In that superb book he talks about your 'mastermind alliance;' your ability to create wealth based upon the team of experts you have around you. Experts who know more than you in other specialised areas.

In Property these masterminds are mortgage brokers, letting agents, estate agents, solicitors, accountants, tax specialists, business coaches and angels and so on. Your skills building relationships will dictate the quality of the people around you. This will proportionately dictate the amount of money you make. Period.

The first thing that you need to do is to educate yourself and read as many Property, sales, marketing, negotiation, business, influence and related books and courses as you can. Go to courses, seminars and networking events.

Side note from Rob: 'If you're 'not really a reader,' then become one! I wasn't a reader at all. The last book I read up until 'Rich Dad Poor Dad,' in 2005 was 'Fantastic Mr. Fox' 13 years previously.

I used to think it was cool that I blagged a 'B' in English Literature at A-Level without reading Chaucer or Shakespeare, it really wasn't; I was just lazy and missed out on an easy 'A.'

Reading wasn't a natural thing for me, it was a learned skill [like so many I've picked up because of my desire to succeed and be wealthy]. It was boring for the first 5 minutes, but get the right book and you don't even notice. I now read a book every 8.3 days. It is just as important as direct experience in my opinion, because **all the answers are out there** for us, we just have to read them and then take action on them.

The traditional road for education would be to go to school, do your GCSE's and A-Levels, go to University for 3-7 years, get a job [where you need experience] and wait 10 years to earn any money.

At one of our courses we were teaching a chap who has been going to Open University for the last 7 years, training to be a Sports Psychologist. He will have to do a couple of years voluntary work before he can really earn to get some credibility, and it will be at least 10 years before he makes any money.

At one point throughout the day I swear he had a mini heart attack, privately to himself. We were going on about leverage and self education and experience and learning and making money as you go along, and he had spent 7 years of his life just to be able to say that he has trained in an industry that is not renowned for making people wealthy.

The more you know, the more you can become an expert in the area of Property. This gives you authority [Law of influence no.5]. You'll be more likely to attract the other experts to you and instill a desire in them to be around you; experts in more niche areas such as finance, tax and the legalities of building a portfolio. Experts who have the skills you need. And remember one of the 'Fundamental tips' from "The 44 Most Closely Guarded Property Secrets?" **Get perfect later**.

I completely and utterly blagged my first job in Property. I had read 3 books and went along to the MD's office of a local Property investment company and proceeded to cheesily quote lines from the 3 books I had read as if I had the actual experience. I don't know to this day if he thought that I actually knew what I was talking about, but the words in those 3 books that I didn't really understand at the time got my big foot in a huge door that has opened a whole host of doors for me. It will continue to do so forever.

The funny thing is that I would have worked for free, but he actually **offered to pay me to learn how to become a millionaire**!

You do need to build on reading though, because it's only the first step up the ladder. You can read all the books in the world but if you stay in your basement and you never take any action, then it's all a big fat waste of your time.

Side note from Mark: talk to people in business and in the business of Property. Network with estate agents, letting agents, brokers, use all of the relationship skills that you learned in "The 44 Most Closely Guarded Property Secrets." Get yourself out there and get people 'on the go.' Offer value and entertain them, have fun, be memorable and many of these doors will open for you like you wouldn't believe.

This book has opened many doors for us: the work we have done with the TV shows: Living, Channel 4, the Business Channel; the articles in The Independent and The Wall Street Journal and the many events we have spoken at. Those in turn have all opened other doors, which will open other doors.

There is an old cliché in the business world: it's not what you know, it's who you know. It's a cliché for a very good reason. This cliché couldn't be more relevant to relationship building and being able to strike up a deal in Property.

Your ability to get 30% below market value deals will be directly proportional to how you build a relationship with your vendor. Let's be honest here, nobody wants to sell their Property at 30% below market value out of choice, so your skills in this area are going to be *the difference that makes the difference*.

Summary

Building relationships is the key to results and success. We can't get away from the fact that we need other people in all areas of successful portfolio building. Build strong and friendly relationships and people will move mountains for you. That's leverage.

Section 5: Motivated Sellers

What is a motivated seller?

The term 'motivated sellers' is a highly used term in the below market value [BMV] Property world.

A 'motivated seller' is someone who wants or needs to sell their Property very quickly and will sell where **price is not their primary concern, driver or motivator**.

The first trick with finding motivated sellers is **in understanding their psychology**. The second trick [using 80/20] is not wasting your time with all of the other sellers who aren't motivated. At first they may seem motivated, but when it comes to the crunch aren't motivated enough to sell around the price you want to buy.

Others you think are motivated may not be in a position right now to be able to sell to you very quickly, at the price you want.

You'll soon be able to filter out the sellers that don't work for your buying rules.

The key concept behind motivated sellers is finding that person, ahead of all the others, who is not hell bent on getting maximum price, who will sell to you where the price is not as important as selling **quickly, discreetly or to someone they trust**.

Fundamental tip No. 3:
The key [Art] to finding a motivated seller is finding a seller who will sell their Property to you where the main driver is not price.
So you get that part. It's clearly very important.

Price is not their primary concern for selling the Property. What 95% of people do is waste 95% of their time trying to persuade unmotivated sellers, or people whose main driver for selling is price, to sell the properties cheap.

They get into a power struggle an energy draining boxing match of a negotiation.

It's not going to work for you. The chances of getting deals that way are so slim. It's certainly not how the professionals do it. You're going to waste your time. If you do finally manage to twist their arm, break their leg, pin them up against the wall and pull their pants down to get them to sell their Property at 30% below market value, when you've left they're only going to have a huge dose of buyer's remorse and they're going to change their mind.

You need to filter out the 95% of people who aren't motivated, who aren't driven by factors other than price. You need to do that quickly. There's a reasonably easy way to do that, although most people don't know how to do it. In the business we call it 'filtering' or 'pre-qualifying.' Marketing is all about asking the right questions to ascertain the main drivers for the sale. Being hyper time efficient.

Once you know the main drivers for making the sale, you target your marketing or base your negotiating skills around those main drivers. Then you'll attract a win-win situation where you can help someone out of a hole, and they can sell you a Property cheaper than maybe they normally might.

Every single motivated seller's main desire or the main thing that they want when they sell a Property to you, is *speed* [not the drug of course]. They want to sell their Property yesterday.

We're going to go through all of the reasons why people might be motivated in a minute. Speed is a key factor to understand. When you know people need to sell their Property very quickly you have control of the negotiation [negotiation power]. When you have control of the negotiation, your chances of getting the Property at 18-30% below market value dramatically increase.

The people who need to sell their Property fast have an immediate, pressing, desperate need for you. You [being a fast, discreet, trustworthy, honest buyer who always completes on deals] will offer something to a motivated seller that most people can't. It is really important when you build your relationships with agents and the language that you use in all of your marketing.

So you've done some diligence and you're in front of a motivated seller. Well done, that's a big part of the job already done! The great thing about motivated sellers is that they must offer concessions or incentives on price to you, which might be your 18-30% below market value. They have no other negotiation tool. You have many.

If the vendor is motivated or in a desperate situation, you can negotiate favourable terms. You could offer lease options, equity sharing or other special clauses that you might be able to set up that are a little bit more creative. More later in the chapter. This allows you to buy the Property where you may not otherwise have been able to using conventional methods, or have an option to buy the Property in the future at a given price. This may win you a deal over a more traditional, inflexible buyer.

Summary

A motivated seller is someone who wants or needs to sell their Property very quickly and will sell where *price is not their primary concern or driver*. Spend your time wisely finding them and dealing with them only. Forget trying to push unmotivated sellers to sell to you, it will be a waste of your time.

Why are people 'motivated' to sell?

Here are the reasons why people are motivated to sell their Property fast and cheap. These are all the reasons we've ever found in our experience.

Debt

Currently we're in a 'credit crunch' where the economy is a little bit tight [you could say!]. The price of living has gone up considerably; the cost of food, the cost of oil, the cost of amenities. The government can try to hide it, but it's there for all to see. Nearly £1.20 per litre of unleaded, £6.20 for a bottle of water and a medium sized popcorn at the local cinema, £60 for a parking ticket, we could go on but Rob will have a seizure!

And guess what; wages haven't gone up anywhere near in accordance with that. Here is a quote from Times online in March of 2008:

'British workers will be taking home an extra £44 a month on average after this year's pay rises, but families are facing an increase of £148 a month in essential living costs.'

And it doesn't end there:

"Based on figures compiled from the responses of more than 4,000 people, the survey – by uSwitch.com, the independent price comparison service - suggested that the average pay rise in Britain this year would be 3.4%, compared with a 9% rise in household bills."

The level of debt is as high as it's ever been. You don't need more evidence of that, but if you want some simply type in 'highest levels of debt' in Google, we found all sorts of shocking articles there.

Lenders are putting their rates up considerably, and all of this is putting a squeeze on the amount of disposable income that people have. The closer to the repossession stage that the motivated seller you're dealing with is, the more likely you are to buy that Property very cheaply.

We'll go into detail about repossession specifically a little bit later on. Of course if vendors have credit card debt, other loans or second charges against their Property [home] then these factors just stated will squeeze them to the point where they can't afford to keep up with the repayments.

The squeeze comes from all angles: pressure from sentiment, worry and fear. The amount of disposable income they have is reduced because wages are not going up as fast as expenditure. The cost of borrowing is going up. Their situation has dramatically changed from a year ago because of rising interest rates being passed on.

If they don't sell their home very quickly, once the squeeze has become too hard, they will start to fall behind and default on some of their repayments. Lenders are going to recall their loans which they can't pay, and they're going to have their house repossessed. And the lenders aren't nice about this. This is business and they want their money. It's in their house, and they're going to take it.

Someone only needs to fall behind for a couple of months on their mortgage and their credit is in big trouble. It's court time.

Divorce

This can change people's circumstances **very quickly**. As you may know, legal expenses can rack up [according to the FT, 50% of you who have been married should know!]. We know people who have spent 6 figures on a divorce settlement. Divorce can be crippling financially, but also if a couple have split up and fallen out [pretty likely to happen, don't you think. Shaking hands, kissing and making up doesn't really happen here!], then the memories attached to their home may not be so pleasant.

They may be fighting for half of the share of the money [or more]. They're going to want to sell that Property very quickly because they just don't want the hassle, the grief, the pain, and to look at that cheating face again!!

Again we've experienced this first hand [not our divorce] and we've bought from people who've been going through divorce. It's messy, but there is opportunity out there. You'd be surprised at how much of a discount people will take on their Property just to get their money out quickly and be rid of the bastard!!

Relocation

Someone may have just bought a new home. When people are looking for new places they get quite excited. If they find their dream home they just want to buy it. We are emotional creatures and many people [not all] will buy on impulse. If the seller is in a chain where they're buying or have just bought their new home, but they still own their old home, they'll need to sell their old home first. Most people can't afford to have 2 homes or 2 mortgages.

If the seller has already bought a new house, they may be driven to sell their old house very quickly so they can get into their dream home. They don't have to spend 3 months paying 2 mortgages.

It might be job relocation. The vendor may be emigrating. There can be many reasons for relocation and it's up to you to find out if they need to **relocate fast**. Very often in job relocation you may not be given 12 weeks' notice to sell or rent out your Property and sort out the hundreds of things that need to be done.

A lot of people don't want to be dealing with a Property when they're miles away from it and may prefer to sell their Property, fast, before they go, where price may not be the main driver. Speed of sale may be more important. Someone may have been sacked from their job or employed by a competing company and have to move on. These are all factors that you want to be looking out for.

You will also want to check with the vendors if other buyers have tried to buy their Property. Deals don't always go through first time around. We've personally bought properties 6 months or a year later, when 2 or 3 deals have 'fallen out of bed,' where buyers have fallen through or pulled out for whatever reason.

If someone is trying to sell their Property for the third time, the pain [a lot of these things are driven by pain] of having to go through another sale falling through may be very high. Stress and emotion can cause us to make decisions that we wouldn't normally make when level and calm. They may decide to sell cheaply if you can buy quickly, and you can guarantee this.

Bankruptcy

This is related to debt and repossession. If people become bankrupt then their Property will be taken from them [as well as many other possessions]. If you can catch them at the right time, you're going to be able to buy that Property for much cheaper than what it's worth because the main motivator is *speed of sale*.

Death in the family

If someone who owns a Property dies or the Property goes into probate, then there's an opportunity to help someone to a desired result and buy a Property at much cheaper than market value.

'But surely buying deceased estates at a discount is not ethical?!'

Well it's not if you steal it from an 87 year old widowed granny, but because you'll offer a better, faster more trusting sale than anyone else, you can both get your desired outcome.

If someone in the immediate family has died; a relative or a partner and not just the primary owner, a lot of pain can be attached to the sale and the person may just want to sell up and move. Speed, trust and discretion will be a higher motivator than price more often than not [if you have pre qualified them].

They may also have the IHT men in black at their door. They aren't the most patient of people, and if you owe inheritance tax you will have to find it with immediate effect. This could force a fast sale.

A birth in the family

If someone has a 2 bed house and they have 2 kids, and then they go and do it again and have another one [when they said they never would], then all of a sudden they don't have enough space to house their new child.

The child won't wait, and it won't give you time and space. When it drops it drops and it needs your full time, space and attention.

In this instance a vendor will need to 'trade up.' This is reasonably common and we've bought properties in this instance. When you have a baby, you have a baby. You can't just sit around and wait. Anyone who has had one will know. Oh we've got it all to look forward to!

Speed: to move out of that Property very quickly will certainly be of the essence; an opportunity for you to work with. Children ain't cheap! Two mortgages aren't cheap either!

Side note reminder: when you are finding motivated sellers, you want to find out which one of these scenarios is relevant for the vendor as quickly as you can [whilst building your rapport]. It's something that you probably will have done [or should have done] before you go to the Property having already had a chat with them. How to blow your leads in one second flat: start talking to people about debt who don't have debt problems.

Distressed landlords

Someone may have bought a couple of investment properties and not realised the work involved, thinking that it would just be a case of 'buy, let out and everything will be fine I'll fall asleep and make millions, Rodney.' These are new or 'speculative' investors.

Being a landlord brings implications and challenges that you have to overcome, just like any business; it's simple, but not easy.

We very often find landlords who are distressed, with anywhere between one and 200 properties in their portfolio. They don't like the hassle and pain, maybe they decided to do all of the management themselves instead of trying to find a letting agent. Maybe they underestimated the size of the task, maybe they bought too many too quickly, maybe they bought too many all over the place like the investor we know who bought 86 all over the UK. They caused him a lot of pain financially and emotionally, and ultimately he lost the portfolio.

Distressed landlords can be a very good source of leads and a great leverage of your time if you can buy many properties in one go. We have also met disgruntled landlords who have been in the business a while and have a good amount of equity. They may be prepared to sell their whole portfolio at a greatly reduced price to ease the pain or the worry of a downturn. You can profit from that.

Many 'old-fashioned' landlords manage their portfolio [rent, maintenance] themselves. If we did it that way for 20 years, we'd throw in the towel and sell up too!

You might think that landlords aren't going to take a 20% hit, but if they are worried about a further drop and, if they have 50 properties at 30% loan to value, it becomes an attractive option to sell up. Selling 10, 20 or

50 properties to the same person is far easier than selling 50 to 50 different buyers. They may have a more 'traditional' view of the market and not see leverage the same way you do. They may be at the end of their investment career and not at the beginning!

There are always opportunities to those who are looking.

Inheritance

You may find a family or an individual who has inherited a portfolio from a deceased relative. Now we're not all born Property investors and very often in this situation, especially if there is more than one person who is the beneficiary of the estate [that can cause conflicts and arguments and opportunities], the beneficiaries may want to liquidate rather than keep the portfolio to release some or all of their money.

If there's more than one beneficiary, they may want to sell very quickly. To do that they will probably have to sell below market value as those IHT men in black will be on their case [again].

Broken chain

If properties that are supposed to be going through don't go through, or are taking an eternity to go through, and you've got someone buying at one end having to wait, and someone selling at the other end causing a delay [or vice versa], then patience starts to erode. Mortgage offers get changed or pulled, estate agents get tetchy and things start to go south.

You'll be able to take advantage. You can help a vendor out who is waiting on an unreliable or inexperienced buyer. The more people that are in the chain, and the longer that chain has been dragging out, the more leverage you will have because of the increased levels of pain.

This is about helping people to their desired outcomes. Here is the 'helping others to achieve their desired outcomes model,' lean in a little, this one is a secret!

First identify their desired outcomes, restate them so that you both know that it is clear and they know that you understand, then do what you can to help them to their desired outcomes, reminding them along the way that you are doing exactly as they want.

Really, most people [99/1] don't understand this.

If their desired outcome is that they need to sell their Property because they've been let down and they need to do it quickly, that's what you're going to be able to help them do; and you're going to tell them that that's what you're doing.

Interesting statistic: one in 3 properties fall through in the UK as an average. When you're dealing with hugely below market value sales as landlords in the buy to let market, that fall out of bed rate can be as much as 50%. Think about this; when you're buying properties and your goal is to buy 20-30% below market value, you're going to get more buyers' remorse, far more so than if you're buying properties at the asking price. Therefore that national average for one in 3 properties falling out of bed across the country is far higher through the investment market.

Knowing those figures keeps you in the game. Even if you haven't got the last Property at your desired price, you know that there's a 50% chance that Property's going to come right back on the market at some stage later on. This is called big picture thinking. There is a bigger picture in all the day to day things you do in the Property world, and it is just as important as the smaller details and 'secrets.'

Summary

The single most important thing to remember when buying Property is to deal with motivated sellers only. You need to find people who are desperate and will sell their home to you on factors other than price. Find what is important to them [speed, discretion, trust, guarantee of sale] and they will sell below market value. Don't waste your time trying to persuade people who don't want to be persuaded.

Questions to ask to find motivated sellers

Before you even view a Property, or before you decide to speak to someone and spend your valuable time trying to do a deal, you will need to ascertain whether they are motivated. That hasn't made you fall off your chair or sun lounger because you know that already!

There are essential questions that you need to ask to save you time and make you money. We've actually created a script for you in this book with the fundamental questions, which you can find at the back on page 392.

You could go into huge amounts of detail but that's irrelevant at this stage because all you are looking to do is ascertain whether it's worth your time to go and see them. You'll need to know the basics:

The address and postcode of the Property

You'll want to be able to do your research right off the bat. If you've got the address and the post code then you can go onto Rightmove.co.uk and you can do your research and diligence.

Find out what that Property is valued at, listed at, or could be sold for on the open market.

Do not believe what the vendor tells you their Property is worth. This is a fundamental mistake that a lot of people make. However, you must ask this question because it's very important. For example, if you ask a vendor how much they think they Property is worth and they think it's

£150,000, and you go and do your research and it's really worth £120,000. You know there's a challenge at hand!

You know that they're going to have to let that Property go at £90,000 for you to buy it. If they think it's worth £150,000 then that's a perceived reduction for them of almost 50%. Very likely that that's a bridge too far.

An important distinction: remember that value can be defined in many [different] ways. We would define value as what the market determines the value is [what the market will pay], but of course value can also be determined by what you believe a Property is worth, what the vendor believes a Property is worth, what a solicitor or a surveyor believes a Property is worth. They'll all be very different figures indeed looked at from a different mindset and from a different level of risk.

Particular details

Name, email and telephone number. You'll need to be able stay in contact with vendors. If the deal doesn't happen right now, you can still contact them in the future, because you know the statistics don't you?!

We very often use marketing to contact people because there's many deals that we try and do that we don't get, and it takes 6 or 7 negotiations for us to get one deal. These figures [that we are always trying to improve] are actually pretty good because we do our filtering up front. If we didn't we'd be getting one in 50 or 60, and that's not a good use of our time. If we weren't buying at 30% below market value we'd probably have a 90% success rate.

Knowing that 50% of sales fall out bed, we want to be able to continually contact vendors and let them know that if they didn't agree a deal with us and they agreed a deal with someone else and it fell through, that we would be able to be there right away. We will *buy quickly, efficiently, discreetly* and in a manner that would suit them.

The [real] reason for selling

This is the golden question where you get to find out their motivation [or at least you get the process started].

Remember that when dealing with vendors, especially motivated vendors, they won't always tell you the truth! You can't take what they say to be the Law [or the truth], because if people are in debt and in really sensitive circumstances, they're only going to tell you the truth if they *really trust you*.

It's very unlikely that they trust you yet, so your job is to build up that level of trust.

You need to find out the reason why they're selling their Property. From that you need to ascertain if that reason is valid, real, or true, and if it isn't how you go about finding out that truth. You can filter what they're saying to find out the real truth; you will be getting very good at that!

When my girlfriend [Rob] says I'm fine. I'm fine. I'm fine. Really I'm fine. Honestly, I'm fine. No. I'm fine. I know I have to do some digging! I've become quite good at filtering that process of answers and I understand that the truth is in there somewhere and she's not telling me it yet!

Rob Moore & Mark Homer

How do I know? Well of course I know her, as you will get to know your vendors. I've seen it before, as you will have when you've dealt with enough vendors, I can read her face and her body language and her tone of voice, and other such telling signs, as you'll be able to too.

We've often had cases where people have told us their reasons for selling their Property and the truth has been quite a long way from their initial commentary! We generally find out the truth right at the point when trust is established. If people are in debt they won't always tell you everything up front:

'Nice to meet you my name is Keith and I'm £60,000 in debt and I've over spent and I'm not good at managing money and the guys who look like the Men in Black have already been around after my sofa that I bought on hire purchase.'

Not very likely, it's a sensitive subject, but of course it's something that you need to know about.

What is their 'situation?'

You need to learn more about the seller's circumstances as to why they got in this position.

Did a member of their family die, are they moving away, have they up or down graded, is there a chain involved, do they want to emigrate and leave the country, do they need to go tomorrow, have they sold everything they've got and the house is empty and that's the last thing they need to sell, are they getting divorced?

All of the different circumstances that lead sellers to become motivated are discussed in the next chapter.

How quickly would they like to sell?

I personally [Mark] like to ask how quickly they would like to sell as I like to get a feeling that price is not their motivating factor early on. By asking how quickly do you want to sell your Property? You're looking for is the following, or something like it:

'Well I've had 2 or 3 people before you who've tried to buy the Property and it didn't go through and it's annoying me now and I'm desperate to sell really fast. If I don't sell really fast I'm going to get repossessed.'

That would certainly prick your ears up, wouldn't it? Now it won't always come out like that. It could come out like:

'Well actually I don't need to sell it quickly at all I thought I'd just stick it on the market and see what happens. I want full asking and I'm prepared to wait to get it as I know what it's worth.'

In this case [unless you think they are blatantly lying, but why would they?] take their email address, phone number, thank them very much, contact them again in 3 months when their perceptions and expectations of the market may have changed.

Important note: keep the questions simple and keep the questions as they are in the script because they're open ended questions. They're open ended for a reason. Inducing 'Yes' and 'No' answers isn't going to tell you very much! You're hoping to coax and eloquently coerce the real answers out of the vendors [more in the negotiation section].

How long has the Property been on the market?

This is an add on from the last question to help you determine how motivated they are.

If the Property has been on the market for a day then the vendor might not be that motivated. If it's fallen through 5 times and been on the market for 18 months and they're in a huge amount of debt, then you may be with a motivated seller, and it might be a good use of time to pursue this lead.

What is their perceived value of the Property?

This is a very important question. It is nothing to do with your research; you already know what the Property is worth.

You use this question to gauge what perception the vendor has of the market. How realistic are their perceptions? How likely are they to want to take a drop on the price? Is it worth spending time with them now or will you have to let the market reduce their expectation over time?

How long have they lived there?

You want to know this to get an understanding of the attachment they may have to the Property, emotionally and financially.

If they've lived there a year, then they're not going to have much emotional attachment. If they're 25 years; in the same village working in the same job 3 minutes walk away [a specific example we have experienced], then they're going to do everything they can to keep that Property. That gives you negotiation power.

They are also more likely to have substantial equity in the Property the longer they have had it. If they have lived there 18 months, you are probably wasting your time.

That said, someone may have second charges and secured loans on their Property, and you will want to find this out upfront.

You can research it in the Land Registry landregistry.gov.uk/houseprices. For £3 you can get a register for the Property giving you the details you need. You can find out the purchase date and you can find out the date when charges were put on the Property.

Looking at the name of the charge holder will tell you if it's a mortgage lender. If it is you'll be able to compare the charges to the value. If it's a debt or finance company, you will have information power [more later in the negotiation section].

Other loans on that Property will need to be fulfilled at sale before they can release equity and put their hands on their money, and this will have a bearing on your ability to do a deal.

What is their mortgage on the Property?

Some people don't always ask this first off but I like to know straight away. My time is important so I pre-qualify as early as I can.

If their Property is worth £105,000 and their mortgage is £90,000 and they have a second charge on it then you know they're not going to be able to afford to sell their Property at £75,000! It will be a waste of your time. Many people who are in debt are leveraged up to their eyeballs. It's a sorry state, but it's 80/20 or 99/1 and that's the reality.

They can't afford to sell their Property at the price you want to pay even if they wanted to sell it to you at that price. You must know up front the mortgage and some details of the loans that they have on that Property. We've had cases where vendors have lied [or didn't know or understand] about second charges and other secured loans.

Are they aware of any problems with the Property?

This is very important for you to know. It is also a good gauge of how truthful the vendor is. You should never take their word for it. Take a surveyor or builder with you when you have pre-qualified, to make sure that everything is as it should be.

We always like to extract as much information as we can without probing too hard and breaking rapport. You are looking for damp, electrical problems, structural issues, problems with neighbours, lease issues, covenants and a feeling for the area.

Summary

There is a process of questioning that will dramatically increase your chances of engaging motivated sellers to sell to you well below market value. You need to ascertain quickly if the sellers are motivated to maximise your time and increase your return.

Where & how to find motivated sellers

The common misconception is that there is no one out there in the market in their right mind [who doesn't live in a nuthouse] who's going to sell you their Property at 30% below market value.

This is a belief. This is not a reality, it is a perception. Last year we had this belief to a small degree. We thought it was certainly a big challenge to buy 30% below market value because we were in a rising, seller's market. The competition was hot and we hadn't done it [yet].

There were more buyers than sellers a year ago. Sellers could trade buyers against each other. It really was quite difficult to get anything above a genuine 15% discount, and very often we'd have to buy at 12% discount and add another 5-8% through the refurb, spending £1 to get £3, to make the deal work.

The market has changed; this is what this book is about. We are finding **more and more motivated sellers**. We bought 11 properties in 10 days in one purple patch in March '08 and these deals are everywhere; **everywhere to those who are looking** for them and who understand how to find them.

The 80/20 principle states that most people will be looking in the wrong place. 80% of the wear is in 20% of the carpet. Well you don't want to be walking on that 20%! That's just the way it goes.

Now we're going to list out all the different methods we know of to find below market value properties and motivated sellers.

Very important point: if you use just 2 of these strategies, if you focused on one strategy as your main strategy, and used 2 or 3 ancillary strategies and totally ignored the rest, you would still find 30% below market value Property deals. The choice here is huge, be creative and try them; they work.

The Internet

We own and run a lead generation site called No More Debt Now nomoredebtnow.co.uk which generates motivated sellers for us and our investors/clients. It's a reasonably simple website, it gives some free information to people which is essential to them in their situation [the Law of reciprocation: builds trust] and it generates questionnaires and interest from people who want to sell their Property.

You can use natural search or SEO [search engine optimisation] to rank your site as high up as you can on Google or other search engines, but that's a long term plan. It costs a lot of money and takes a lot of time. Most people think SEO is free because you don't physically pay to get on the page, but to get anywhere near where anyone can see it will cost you a lot of money and time. Friends of ours have lead generation sites that have cost them over £300,000 to develop. You would also need to have been in the business or in your niche for a very long time.

You can use Google Adwords or other cost-per-click/pay-per-click engines [CPC/PPC], and we'll talk a little more about that in the marketing section. This is a very effective strategy. It can be reasonably expensive to generate leads but as you get better you'll generate more and more for a lower and lower cost. You are rewarded for being better than the competition, which is exactly what we want.

There are a lot of leads to be found on the Internet. More and more people have access to the internet; pretty much every house has an internet connection. That's a big pond to fish in!

Estate agents

This is our preferred method and our most prolific strategy. We've been working on relationships with estate agents for around 4 years. We have the time in the market, the experience, we've built the personal relationships; we have the trust.

In our opinion estate agents are the best source for deals, based on our application of 80/20 and our personal experience, but like anything else it takes a bit of time up front. But so does the internet, leafleting, postcarding, and any other strategy for generating leads.

I've never seen anyone meditate or sit at home watching Corrie and have a bag of money fall on their head.

If we're realistic here, when you generate leads through the internet you know that you have to put up a reasonable amount of money to build your site and get it optimised and ranked and in the right places to be seen on the right keywords before you get any calls.

Estate agents don't just run to you with 30% deals, get on their knees, kiss your feet and beg that you take them off their hands! We meet a lot of people who just say:

'I'm not going to deal with estate agents, it's too much time it's too much effort,' and they go off and pay a load of finders a bag full of money [that didn't drop out of the sky] to generate 'leads.'

They know nothing about those leads and they're dependent on those finders. If you spend some time, it could just be a few hours a week or 3 hours on a Saturday, to build relationships with every single estate agent in your area, you are going to start a very important process rolling. Sure, not everyone's going to bring you the deals that you want right away, but if you've got good relationships with 20 estate agents then your ability to generate leads is going to be significantly increased. That is certainly better than 20 finders in our experience.

It's great from a marketing perspective too. Let me explain [Rob]: in marketing you have 2 strategies to find leads [customers/sellers/deals], one is known as 'push' and one is known as 'pull.'

A *push* strategy is where you go out and you hand out leaflets and you stand on street corners and shout and you walk from door to door and you're trying your best to get people to buy from you and your dragging them by their collars and coat tails to buy your product or take the action that you want them to take. It's very time intensive and a very low return on time investment. It has its place, and it is where everyone starts. The more proactive you are, the better return you will get from your push strategy. However, common problems are the amount of time it takes and people's lack of rejection proofing.

If you build relationships with estate agents steadily you build up trust with them. You do everything that you say you're going to do, you go on viewings when they need you to, you think of what they want, then you'll create a *pull* strategy. After the initial platform building you can sit at home or in your office and you'll get phone calls from estate agents who will bring you deals. It does happen, like a tidal wave that starts miles out at sea and gets gradually bigger and bigger until the point where it hits the shore with power and size and authority [and floods the town].

Do not underestimate the value of using estate agents. It's been our best strategy for many years. We spend lots of time and money leafleting, internet marketing and on a whole host of other strategies we talk about in this book, and still estate agents are the best for us for generating deals [not just leads].

Mail drops

Leafleting, postcarding or putting slips in newspapers that get delivered to strategically targeted properties.

This strategy can be very good, but you need to know your numbers and you need to understand that it is going to cost you some cash. It can be a blanket strategy; like chucking bits of paper out of a plane and hoping a couple will land on the right house. It's not always the most efficient and there's a low return.

If you get a 0.1% return on the amount of leaflets that you deliver, then you're doing pretty well. You can mass print leaflets reasonably cheaply,

180 www.progressiveproperty.co.uk

you can get them delivered reasonably cheaply and they can be an effective strategy if you use economies of scale.

The [important] points of note in leafleting strategy are as follows:

Your marketing copy needs to be so good on your leaflets that when someone picks it up they are compelled to give you a ring. You have to make that call to action irresistible. You need to make it so compelling that they'll get up in the middle of the night, walk 100 miles in the rain in their dressing gown just to pick up the phone, meet you or take the action that you desire.

This might sound a little over the top, and yes the reality is that most people aren't going to do that, but the point is differentiation. Why should I even bother to call you over anyone else? What have you got that I want or need? What can you do for me?

The words you use must create trust, interest, desire, traction and commitment. In marketing the model or formula is AIDA: Attention, Interest, Desire, Action.

The first part is ATTENTION! Heeellllo?! WAIT! STOP!

OK, so you have my attention now!

The second part is Interest. You can shout and scream and jump up and down all you like, but if you don't create interest, you'll be ignored. Many people are good at the Attention part but don't then create the **necessary interest to keep attention.**

Rob Moore & Mark Homer

In the modern world we all have the attention spans of Goldfish. You need to be good at creating interest. Once you have a captive, interested vendor or lead, you then need to create **D**esire. You need to make them want what you have or what you offer. If you can make them desire so much that they need it, it will be even more effective.

And then commitment to **A**ction. The worst thing in the world for you as a buyer would be to do all the hard work creating AID and then letting someone else in to do the deal and take the money. Many people fear the most important part: *asking for the money*.

The next thing about leafleting [and the biggest mistake people make] is that they chuck a load of leaflets out all over the shop. They deliver 50,000 in a month all over the place. They get 3 calls and none of them become a deal, so they decide that leafleting doesn't work.

People who are new to Google Adwords will use 'short-tail' generic keywords that are never going to generate them any deals, spend a grand and then say 'Google Adwords doesn't work.'

You have to persistent with your leafleting campaign. It is a strategy not a one hit wonder. Anyone who has studied marketing will know that the average number of times someone needs to be asked a question before they'll take any action is 7 times; a 7 time convincer strategy. Using that theory, if you deliver a leaflet to a house 6 times, then averages state that the recipients aren't going to take a blind bit of notice.

Our strategy for leafleting: we only leaflet in the areas that *we know have the highest yields* [80/20]. We only leaflet in the areas we have bought in before, we know, and are tested [unless we are trailblazing]. That's 4 or 5 micro-economies of Peterborough, and we will leaflet in those areas heavily every week.

We'll make sure that those houses get 7, 10, 15, 20, 50 leaflets. It might take 20 or 50 times to convince someone and get them to take an action; **when it is right for them**. Statistics state that only 1-3% of people will be ready to buy your product now. The other 97 - 99% may be ready sometime in the future, or they may be able to be convinced.

You have probably been offered or invited to buy this book 5-40 times before you actually bought it. We believe that it is worth our time if this book makes a difference to you in any way.

Persistence is key. However if you're persistent in areas where properties are £200,000 and the yields are 4%, then even if you do get a call, it's not going to matter because you're not going to get a deal that's any good.

Instead of sending 50,000 all over your town, send 10,000 leaflets at a time in 3-5 areas where **you know you're most likely to get the deals.** Where the deals are proven for you, where you know you would buy, where the yields are high, and the values are relatively low.

Again we're using the 80/20 principle religiously.

Delivery: this is something we had huge problems with. We found it so hard to find a trustworthy source to deliver our leaflets. We paid big mail-order companies significant amounts of money to do mass drops. We've put leaflets in newspapers, given them to paperboys, we've tried all sorts of strategies and many of them haven't worked.

The reason we know this is because we **test**. You already know how vital testing is, having read "The 44 Most Closely Guarded Property Secrets." We own many of the properties in the areas we leaflet to and we go in and check them regularly. You must go and check that your leaflets are being delivered.

You can be the best marketer in the world, get the printing at the best price, get a great compelling message and write awesome sales copy. You could highly personalise the leaflets to make them seem hand delivered and written personally, but if they don't get through the letter box, then it's all a total waste.

In our experience huge mail order companies do not always deliver as they should. If you buy lists of addresses you are taking a risk because many of them may not be pre-qualified or they may be outdated. Many leafletters aren't really that bothered or driven to drop your leaflets [no matter how good your relationship skills are].

Let's be honest here it's not a golden, dream, once in a lifetime job. It's not particularly interesting and it takes a certain type of person to deliver consistently for you, pounding the streets day after day after day; someone who does care, but might not have aspirations to be a businessman or businesswoman. Someone who is happy and content and has simple desires.

You may be able to get a newspaper deliverer or a paperboy to stick some leaflets in newspapers, but our guess [and experience] is that most of those won't get delivered. The best type of person we have found for delivering leaflets effectively [though you will have to set the expectation in terms of performance] are 25-45 year old women, possibly unemployed, or full time mothers that can't really work as much as they would like to and require flexible working hours. This is the demographic of person who you can **trust**, aren't likely to find a better job next week and are **happy with consistency** and **desire security**.

A good friend of ours with whom we work closely, who has over 80 properties, has a great strategy that works for him. He speaks to doctors and asks what remedies they have to help people combat obesity. Once he is in and has built rapport he asks if the doctors will get the patients to go out and deliver leaflets for him! No lie! How unbelievable [and genius] is that?!

They are prescribed 'leaflet dropping' as a remedy.

This works well for him and it just shows that you can be as creative with these strategies as you want to be. You are only limited by what you believe [or don't believe].

Delivering leaflets yourself for the long term is Mickey Mouse. It's not a great strategy for leverage and you'll end up hating it, but it's a very good idea to do the first 5,000-20,000 yourself so you know how it works. You have a good grasp on the number of responses you should be getting.

Go around the areas, get a feel for them, work out roughly how long it takes you to deliver 500 at a time [we have experienced anywhere between 200 and 350 per hour] and translate that into the number of calls you get. Doing 50 or 100 won't give you good enough data, so you need to get out and about a few weekends and find out how it all works.

We have a strategy for business which has served us well. Any new venture we go into, we always do the work ourselves first. It may just be basic groundwork, like testing areas by delivering leaflets yourself, or it might be writing your first book and self publishing it so you know how the process works for next time when you sub contract things out. People will take the piss if you let them, so you need to know a little about what they are doing for you, so you can keep control and so people don't pull the wool over your eyes.

You'll just know straight away, using this strategy, if the leafletters are chucking them in a skip or a river.

Classified ads

Using the local newspaper, if done correctly and incrementally, can generate a lot of interest; *hot leads ready to sell Property*.

However this strategy can burn money fast and a lot of our research suggests that ads can cost £400-£500 for an ad of reasonable size. Many publications [even local ones] will demand that you pay for 12 supplements up front; you could be looking at £6,000! This can be very expensive so you absolutely need to know that you're going to get a return on your investment [ROI].

Another cheeky little strategy that has worked well for us is what we call the 'cheque hook.' Get in touch with publications, build some rapport with them and get their prices. Find out when ads go to print and the deadlines for submissions. Once you know this send a cheque first class 48 hours before the deadline with a comp slip.

Send your ad around 12-24 hours before the deadline. If you have been given a quote for £300 for an ad for a week, then write the cheque for £125. On the comp slip you sent with the cheque write:

'Dear Sally,
Please find enclosed a cheque for £125 for the ad as agreed under the following conditions [add your conditions: place of ad, duration, etc]. Many thanks indeed. Please could you contact me in the future about further ad placements.'

It should land on their desk at around the same time as your ad. Clearly, the cheque is not the quoted price, and this will not always work, but many times the publication will simply cash the cheque and place your ad. If there are any gaps in the ad space at all [which there always is] then cash in the bank is good for them, especially now when they may be finding business a little tough.

This little beauty has worked for us a good few times.

Personally, we don't just want to test ads in publications where we're going to pay £6,000; we want to know upfront that these adverts are going to deliver results. A good way to do this is 'scraping'. Someone who came to one of our presentations calls it 'benchmarking.'

You might call it copying! I [Rob] used to think that copying was for cheaters or followers, and was obsessed with creating something new every 10 minutes. The problem with that strategy is that it takes forever, and 99% of the time you're never going to succeed. In the NLP world it is known as 'modelling.' There's a whole section on this later in the book.

Remember the Sam Walton story from before? He was an absolute master at modelling his competition. He spent a great deal of his time in his competitors' stores copying the things that worked for them. And it worked for him!

So before you throw 6 grand at one ad that could bring you nothing, test on a smaller scale using a platform such as Google adwords where you can test marketing copy at a fraction of the price. Scrape, benchmark, copy or model advertising and marketing that works [or appears to work based on what you know].

Perhaps that might be ads that you've already seen in the paper [local, national, Yellow Pages]: ads that have been in the paper for the last 3 to 9 months. You want to get yourself a swipe file of all the good marketing material you find. Save online 'copy' [text/ads/sales pages] to your favourites. Keep all the direct marketing you get through the post, and every time you go to Tesco read the headlines of the glossy magazines. Love 'em or hate 'em, the glossy women's magazines know how to write headlines that make you stop and want to open them.

This will **save you time and money**, and will give you a reference point when you start new ads and campaigns. We don't do anything now if we can get someone else to do it or we can model other people before us to **save time and money**.

You'll also start to notice a couple of things. For example if you kept every Property paper or every local rag for 6 months and went through each week, you would notice some of the ads that are there week in week out [probably making money] and you would notice many of the ads that go in for a month then go again, then go in for a month then go again [probably not making money].

When you 'scrape' you want to make sure that you don't copy something that doesn't work. You will find ads that have been in there one or 2 years. People aren't going to leave an ad in a paper if it's £400 a time for 6 years if it doesn't work and it doesn't bring a return on investment. Blatantly obvious we know, but how many people actually do it? [99/1].

We mentioned testing on Google Adwords just a few moments ago, and this is a little secret tip for you that will save you time and money and hold you in good stead for many marketing years to come. The title of this book, the title of our last book and a lot of the marketing we use comes from testing on Google Adwords. For a small amount of money, 5-50 pence a click, you can test headlines, body copy, landing pages and full page ads. Make all the mistakes you want; it's not going to bankrupt you.

You can test and see what kind of conversions you get. Once we've tested our copy on Adwords; 10 to 20 ads against each other, and we've found the best ad that produces the best return on investment or the most leads, then we know we can convert and upscale to print media [and any other media]. We know it'll convert because the psychology of influence and laws of marketing are no different when speaking, looking on the screen, to reading in the paper to the printed word. The rules will always be the same.

Google Adwords is a fantastic tool because you can control the amount of money that you spend. You can test your advertising media before you upscale. Don't get talked into expensive lead generation.

Doctors

Another good source of leads. This is where you find out where people become ill [some of our secrets really are groundbreaking, aren't they?!].

But seriously, you can post marketing and lead generation material in doctors' surgeries. You have a captive audience of patients and friends and families of patients. Doctors are always late and people get bored waiting. You've probably read all sorts of crap at the Doctors like a 10 year old copy of 'People's Friend.'

Our Doctors have now moved into the digital advertising world. There may be opportunities for you to utilise this new medium of advertising. Doctors are perfect for that because you have no real choice other than to read what is there [unless you like sterilised white walls].

Just to reiterate a very important point that you already know; you are not there like a vulture waiting for people to kick the bucket so you can take their family to the cleaners and laugh like Dr. Evil! You are simply looking for opportunities to help other people with their *challenges and problems* in a way that also works for you both.

Accountants

Accountants deal with people and they understand their financial situations. Accountants will know of people in financial predicaments.

All you need to do in these specific places such as doctors and accountants is put up small posters in as many lobbies and foyers as you can. People are going to be seeing your adverts in multiple areas, and those 7 time convincers are going to be fulfilled and you're going to get far more returns and far more calls, and you're going to **make more cash**.

Marketing is about mindspace. It's about getting in someone's mind. Coca Cola and Virgin; they'll hit you 100's of times [literally] a day. If they only hit you once a day you'd never buy Coke you'd go with Pepsi and you'd never go with Virgin you'd go with Sky. Awareness, association and **mindspace** will **generate desire and action**.

The more times you 'hit' someone's mind and get **top of mind awareness**, the more they'll think of you when selling their house. Your name comes right at the top of their mind, before anyone else. You're going to make money. That's when you go from an accidental or novice to a seriously leveraged skilful investor.

Solicitors

Like accountants, you have professionals who deal with people and they understand people's financial and legal situations. If you can build relationships with doctors, solicitors, accountants, mortgage brokers, and bridging lenders; people who have a databases, then you are creating a very powerful mastermind alliance that you are leveraging, that are working for and with you to help you achieve your goals.

Mortgage Brokers

You'd be amazed at the amount of great mortgage brokers there are who have databases of Property buyers and sellers; people who've all asked and shown genuine interest in Property; 'I want to sell Property, I want to raise a loan on my Property.' There's no messing about here, you know they are interested. They are highly filtered leads and you will be playing on the right side of the 80/20 principle.

Auctions

This is a very specific strategy which seems to come and go in terms of its effectiveness. In a rising market we find that auctions become less and less effective for us. Since Property Ladder and Homes Under the Hammer and all of these fashionable TV shows [eye candy for the general public], it seems that every Tom, Dick and Harry [every accidental or speculative investor] was running along to the auctions to try their hand at the Property game.

Therefore the competition started to influence price. People were bidding on properties thinking they were cheap when they weren't. As a result professional investors were getting outbid in the market.

This has changed again now that we are in a falling market. The speculative investors, and many mortgaged professional investors, have thrown in the towel at auctions and the competition has dramatically reduced again based on both sentiment and reality.

Because of the nature and the specificity of auctions it rules a lot of people out of the market. A lot of people don't have the money ready and can't do the deals quickly enough. This creates an opportunity for you. It's become easier to find deals at auction because we're in a falling market and most people who go to auctions are cash buyers. There aren't many cash buyers at all in the market now.

We're finding that investors are getting some very good deals from auctions now, so this strategy is something you should seriously think about if you have a little bit of cash and if you understand the process involved.

Like the late 90's and the turn of the 21st century, you can buy bargain properties, repossessions, residential and local government properties and commercial Property through auction. You can also buy some weird and wonderful properties with strange constructions, irregular contracts, leases and planning permissions.

You need to watch out for these. Auction houses can be full of unconventional, un-mortgageable properties that you don't want to be left with: kippers.

Some things to be aware of at auctions:

Auctions aren't necessarily 'fully loaded with Property bargains' like you may be led to believe. A lot of properties are at auction for a reason; they can't sell because they're not good investments. You have to see through all the smoke and have a clear strategy. You can also get bid up by people at auctions. If you ever go into a Property auction with your emotions then you're going to end up losing money.

Homes Under the Hammer and all these Property shows glorified auctions. People just loved the thought of going to auctions and standing there looking like a professional and bidding on properties. They get attracted by low guide prices, and before they know it they're paying market value for a Property that they really need to get 40-50% below to make the numbers work.

Most of these people don't do their research; they're speculative investors and you don't even want to entertain getting into bidding wars with them. Let the Wookie win!

How an auction works

You need to have had a valuation on the Property before you even bid on it. That could be expensive if you are researching a few properties. You will definitely want all of your legals done so that you know what you are getting into if you are serious about buying through auction. More detail as we go through this chapter.

Many people buy Property at auctions without even viewing the Property. Big mistake. It is quite a challenge when buying at auction to get a good enough feel for the Property, the area, the rental market and the vendor because you just don't have enough time beforehand.

What looks good at first or second view could end up being a whole structural project. A vendor who you do not yet have rapport with may hide things from you because they just want the Property sold.

Once the hammer goes down there is no turning back. You will need to put 10% down on the day. If you can't complete in time you don't get that money back. Many auction houses will expect you to complete in 14 days, and most people can't. Some might allow 28 days. Many auction houses also have hidden administration costs that can be 1-2% of the sale price.

Different auction houses have different strategies and rules regarding viewing properties. Some will do block viewings on a Property which isn't always the best and you're not always going to find the best deals that way. Others will request that you ask them and they'll arrange a viewing for you, others may ask for you to arrange viewings or may ask you not to arrange viewings and not to bother the tenant.

This may deter some other investors, so at this point you may see an opportunity. It's really important to go and have a look at the Property beforehand.

There are different ways of doing it. You can't just go up to someone's Property and barge in and say 'let me have a look at your Property now!'. What right do you have? But you may be able to go and introduce yourself as someone who may potentially buy this Property from the auction. Be nice, build rapport, ask for just a few minutes of their time and ask them to tell you a bit about the Property. Try to get them to tell you a few things that may be wrong with it and take a quick look.

Remember that vendors will not always tell you the truth, especially if they are selling their Property through auction.

Get attention and then say something like 'OK that's interesting, in order for me to be able to buy this Property I'm going to need to come and have a look so I can get some kind of assessment and my builder can sort this out so I can become your landlord.'

Get them interested and believing that you could buy that Property. It's in an auction for a reason. It might be that they need to sell the Property very quickly; in fact it's more than likely that this is the case. If they believe that you could become their landlord then they're more likely to let you in and let you have a look round.

Once you're in take a look around, take some photos and note everything in a notebook because you're going to want to know as much as you can upfront. You don't want any surprises.

And don't just go and look at one Property before going to auction and bank on that being your one deal. The chances are you'll get outbid and you won't get that Property. So go and view 5 or 10 properties, do your diligence on all of those properties and bid on 5 that are right and that fit within your rules.

You may then get one deal out of those. You're not going to throw the dart and hit the bullseye first time, every single time.

The seller of the Property will set a reserve price. The reserve price is the minimum price that the seller will allow the Property to be sold for.

The guide price is generally figured out by the auctioneer and the seller to work out a rough estimate of the selling price. The guide price is the starting price as advertised and they'll generally set it low[ish] because they want to attract interest.

They want people bidding against each other. Very often we've seen people who've ended up paying 20% over the market value because they've got in a bidding war, which is something you need to be aware of [and avoid].

As long as the bids come in that are on that reserve price or higher, a deal will done. You'll be asked to exchange on the Property and you'll have to put down 10% of the sale price there and then, upfront.

If a Property doesn't reach the reserve price then it will be withdrawn and it won't be sold through the auction. You may have the opportunity to approach the seller afterwards and perhaps strike a deal. This can be a good way to find properties. Watch for the repossessions that don't meet the reserve and be ready.

Before you go to auction

You'll need to order an auction catalogue. You'll want to know what's coming up in auction so you can do your research. The easiest way to do this is to phone up the auction house and they'll send you a copy of the auction catalogue. They'll also probably try and get you to subscribe to their database and pay a monthly subscription to receive more auction catalogues. You don't actually need to do that.

Most of the time if you phone up 30 days before the auction they'll send you one for free. You can also do your internet based research and if you go to eiggroup.co.uk

This company lists the entire database of Properties to be sold at auction in the entire country and that's a very useful place to do your diligence.

You have to pay a subscription for that but you'll be able to see every single auction Property coming up across the country on that database.

You might go to an auction in London but they'll be selling properties across the country and you should really only be interested in properties within a certain patch that you're working on so that you can keep control of your portfolio.

Don't buy anything out of the ordinary, no matter how good the price might look. Stay away from anything over a restaurant or take away, don't buy a toilet and don't buy any of these weird and wonderful structures with 'potential planning' because they are not proven and they are in an auction for a reason.

Don't go for anything where the price seems to be too good to be true. There is normally a reason for that. Anything ridiculously cheap or 10 properties at £10,000 each on the same street will probably be in an area where you couldn't give them away.

They are likely to be in the very worst areas. Yes, the yield might look attractive but that depends on you renting them out! Your voids and refurb costs could end up making you bankrupt, the area could be under compulsory purchase or the whole area might just need bombing and starting all over again!

Even if you could rent them out you're not going to be dealing with the Jones' when it comes to tenants. You might end up with all your radiators nicked for drug money [yes, it has happened!].

There are a very specific set of rules to buying at auction that a lot of people can't fulfil. You should not enter into a purchase at auction without knowing the process.

It's absolutely essential to set a maximum bid before you even get in that room and stick to it. Obviously having viewed those properties, having done your diligence, having had a valuation, you also need to assess what refurb costs may be involved.

Getting a valuation on a property will highlight certain structural defects and issues but not everything, so it might be a good idea to take a builder or a surveyor with you; a friend who can give you a good idea of how much costs will be involved in doing up the Property once you buy it to get it into a rentable condition.

We would stick a 20% contingency on top of that in case things go wrong, and factor in more time because the unexpected may well happen. You need to factor this all in before you even get in the room and before you set your maximum bid.

Once you've taken all of these into account and you've got what you think is a fair reflection, and you've come up with a price that you believe is the maximum you are prepared to pay, absolutely stick to it. Do not get involved in any bidding wars, don't think oh well it will only be an extra grand or 2, because that will turn into £5,000 and all your profit will be gone.

Preparing for the auction

You need to make sure you give the auctioneer a call a few days before or the day before to make sure that the properties that you are interested are in are still up for auction. They may have been sold or they may have been released from auction so you don't want to waste your time.

Very often you'll get prior bids which will be bid on the Property before the auction takes place. Be wary of what happens here because if the prior bids have gone up quite high then that might give the seller an indication that they can get a good market value for the Property.

Make sure you study the auction catalogue carefully. Read the conditions of sale and any other particulars that may have been included in the catalogue and any amendments, so that you know up front the conditions in which you're buying.

Remember that guide prices can be a bit of a red herring. Just because they're low doesn't mean you're going to get the Property cheap. If they're exceptionally low then you may get a lot of competition from developers, if they are reasonably high then it may also scare off other bidders and scare off competition, and this could be quite good for you. If there's no competition then even if there's a reasonably high reserve or guide price, you might actually get it well under market value because of the lack of other bidders.

On the auction day

Make sure you turn up early, at least one hour before so you can mingle with a lot of the professional investors and serious investors.

You might want to get to know many of them because you might be able to strike up future joint venture partnerships or learn a lot from them. You're not really here competing with people, you're here to build relationships and there are more than enough deals for all of us.

There are some things to be aware of when you turn up on the day. You'll need some identification [passport or driving license] and you'll need the relevant method of payment. Many don't take cheques or cash so you'll need to be able to pay in the right method. This will not be accepted as an excuse after you've won the bid so you need to be able to do that on the day, and that will be your responsibility.

Make sure that you read the legal packs before you go into the bid because it may tell you things about your Property that you didn't know. Read it very carefully. There may be, and can often be covenants and restrictions placed on land and future development that might be near to where you potential Property is situated.

You need to know of any special conditions of sale, and applicable planning permissions, you'll obviously want to see the searches, the office copy entries, copy of the title deeds, any kind of leases that are on the Property or details of past rents [especially if you're bidding with a tenant included]. The history of the rental payments could be a determining factor. These all make a big difference when you bid.

If you don't understand anything it's a good idea to take people with you who do. Some people take developers with them and they'll even take solicitors with them. These people will be able to advise you. Listen to what the auctioneer has to say very carefully because there can be last minute changes in lots.

One of the fundamental mistakes that a lot of people make is they go in and they sit at the front because they want to be close to the auctioneer to see what's happening, but they can't see what's happening because all the action is behind them. You'll notice if you watch TV shows that professional `s will stand at the back with their backs against the wall because they can see the whole room and they can see everybody else who is bidding. They get a good view and a good feel for the atmosphere.

Using the 80/20 principle again, 80% of the people in the room are not there for serious buying, they just want deals that they're never going to get so they're delusional about it. Perhaps they're just beginners trying to learn, they're amateur investors, people without anything better to do, or people who've just watched Homes Under the Hammer. It's really important to understand that you're not competing with most of the people in the room [the myth of competition]. It's probably only 5-20% of the room who are serious bidders with any money to invest.

The bidding process

The auctioneer will give you a signal if you've indicated a bid. It's quite funny, people get scared and think that if they flinch or scratch their nose or rub their eye, that's going to be a bid and you're going to be paying 30% over market value for that Property.

It doesn't work like that; you'll be pleased to know. The auctioneer will need confirmation of a bid, so make it clear. A good tip that can be useful is instead of coming in and bidding at the start which a lot of people do, come in right at the end, just at the point when the Property is about to be sold. It can be quite unnerving and put other bidders off, because at that point he may have fought off a lot of people and thought that they were about to get the Property. All of a sudden you come in.

Don't show any emotion when you're bidding because any weaknesses that you show may be picked up on by other bidders. Keep looking at the auctioneer and don't get involved with any banter with rival bidders. You just want to look relaxed about it. If you look relaxed and comfortable then that's what people believe you are. Very often this will put people off bidding against you.

They'll think you know what you're doing, you've been here before and this is obviously something you're good at. Remember that **perception is reality** so you want to give out the perception that this is what you do every day. Other people are in a similar situation where they haven't done it before and you need to be better than them, even if you're not. Some people will attend auctions by phone and bid by phone. This is not the best strategy. It's like buying a Property without looking at it. You want to gauge a sense of the atmosphere in the room. You want to understand the people you're bidding against.

You can bid on the internet, but it really is best to go to auctions in person because you want to get a flavour for it. You're only going to learn how it works by going. We personally wouldn't bid in auction if we attend it.

Some tricks to watch out for in bidding

'Bidding off the chandelier' is where the auctioneer will take fake bids off people. They're looking to get the price right up to the guide. If you're standing at the back of the room you'll get a good idea of what's going on and if this is happening; you'll be able to see it, but you won`t sitting at the front.

This is another good reason why you don't want to get too emotionally involved in bidding on properties at auction. This is a perfectly legitimate strategy for auctioneers to use but they can't use this after the reserve price has been met. Watch out for these tricks.

Watch out for plants or stooges or shill-bidders; people who have been planted by the auction house to bid against you to bid you up. If you bid on emotion then you could end up paying way over the odds by bidding against someone who had no intention of buying the Property.

If you've done your research and your diligence and you know what you're going to pay then this will never happen to you anyway, but just something to keep your eye on and be aware of.

Paying for the Property

The Property is sold to the highest bidder and if the reserve isn't met then the lot is withdrawn and you can approach the auctioneers and put an offer in after the auction has ended.

The seller may well accept a lower offer under the reserve price if they're highly motivated because they might not want to have to go through the whole process of putting the Property through another auction. It can be costly and time consuming.

Once you've agreed a price on a Property you'll need to pay for it! The rules will ever so slightly vary depending on the auction house, but generally you'll have to put 10% deposit down immediately after the hammer is down and you'll have to complete a maximum of 28 days afterwards. Many of them will demand completion within 14 days and it may not be possible to get a mortgage in this time, so you have to make sure of the special conditions of each and every lot that might be individual or unique.

You can use mortgages to buy properties at auction but again a lot of it depends on the completion time and as you know raising mortgages can take 6-12 weeks. This isn't going to work for a 14 day completion.

A good strategy is to buy cash if you can, remortgage once you've bought to release all of your money out, add value through your refurb and you've bought a Property with no money or even a decent cash back. Other people like to use bridging finance.

You need to have all of these strategies in place, you need to have decisions in principle done, know that the mortgage brokers and solicitors can work quickly and get this through in time, know that the people who are lending you the bridging fund can do it quickly and efficiently so that you can complete in time and you can buy the Property.

Enough about auctions for now!

Adverts

Put them everywhere [mindspace].

Posters

Create loads of posters and put them up in every foyer of every doctor, every accountant, every solicitor, every lawyer, every newsagent, every post office, and every take away [mindspace].

Postcarding

A great little strategy. Write 50 or 100 hundred postcards and every time you go into a newsagent ask them to stick them up in their shop window. Most of them will let you do it for free; every single post office will probably let you do it for free. If they don't they're only going to charge you a small amount of money, well worth a few pounds here and there for a deal or 2, don't you think?!

You've got mindspace. You've got more and more people seeing your advertisements. This is not like throwing a dart in the bullseye straight away. The more darts you throw, the more likely you are to hit the bullseye, and this is what it's all about. You can place postcards and small sticker adverts everywhere. You can put them on cars, on lampposts, on t-shirts, on benches, on buses, on place mats in restaurants; they can go absolutely everywhere.

If you can find low cost methods of advertising [don't spend a load of money on something that's unproven] then do them as much as you can. The ROI on this strategy is huge, and you should be able to get a couple a year this way.

Repossessions

You can get properties about to be repossessed from repossession agents or estate agents who deal with repossession. This has become a fashionable [and good] method for finding leads. You will have to get the timing right on this. If it's gone to the stage of repossession then it might be too late for you to be able to help.

We know a lot of people who spend a lot of time in, outside and around Court`s because that's where you find the people who are actively going through repossession. If you can help them out, advertise, or hand out leaflets where the people are, you could be onto a winner.

A bankruptcy company

Go where people are who are most likely to be able to give you the Property you want at the price you want.

Where do people who have financial difficulties hang out? Where do people who are getting divorced hang out? Where do people who are in a probate situation or deceased estate hang out? What magazines do they read? What do they buy and where do they shop? Get your ideal client profile. The more you know about them and the more you know where they go, what they do, what they eat, where they sleep, what TV they watch; the more likely you are to find them.

Large portfolios

If you can find large portfolios for sale and you know what you know now about the market, then there may be an opportunity to buy large portfolios in one go from investors who may have had enough.

This strategy can save you much time and effort. Instead of spending a lot of time and money on multi marketing strategies to find one deal here and there, if you can find a portfolio of 20 Properties and get 25% off the whole lot. The amount of money you'll save just doing that one deal could be huge.

Surveyors

Surveyors who value properties are going to know the investors in town, they're going to have been and valued properties that might be right for you. When surveyors go round and value properties, they'll see and speak to the vendor, and they may find out information that can help you.

Summary

There are many places to find motivated sellers and cheap properties. The more strategies you utilise, the more deals you will find. Some are time intensive but cheap and others are leveraged but will cost you in marketing pounds. Always keep your eyes open and your ears to the ground. In the current market debt is rife and there are many unconventional ways of finding deals and helping people out of debt.

Repossessions

The statistics for the majority of the population unfortunately do not look good. According to the Council of Mortgage Lenders, over 4,000 estate agents fear that they're going to have to shut the doors of their business across the UK.

Repossessions are expected to move up to 45,000 homes this year which is twice as many as there were in 2007. And it is likely that it will get worse before it gets better. Here is a quote taken from the Citizens Advice Bureau:

'Not only have the number of repossessions increased by 21% in the past year, but the total number, at 27,100, is almost twice the total two years ago in 2005. These increased figures reflect what Citizens Advice Bureau are seeing nationwide. Last year, we dealt with over 57,000 problems about mortgage and secured loan arrears, an 11% increase on the previous year. '

It also goes on to state:

'The actual repossession figures tend to understate the true scale of the problems faced by borrowers at the margins of affordability.'

This is going to have an impact on the Property market and the economy, for sure. It already has.

The opportunity arises for anyone who is liquid. Anyone who realises this opportunity in the market and acts quickly has the potential to buy Property from sellers who are highly motivated. You now know how to find them and how to deal with them in a way that works best for everyone.

Getting to people just before the point of repossession will help them out and give you the *most price negotiation power* and leverage.

Remember there's not much point trying to get a deal once the Property has been repossessed; it's far too late then. However you can deal with repossession companies and repossession specialist estate agents.

Agents will market Property right up to the point of exchange. This has caused us some pain in the past. You might agree a deal well below market value and end up being gazumped. This has happened to us a few times, and sometimes by just £1,000 or £2,000.

Although you have made a deal the 'rules' state that the Property must continue to be marketed to exchange [according to the agents and repo companies]. Your relationships with the agents will be very important in these circumstances.

You're playing a bit of a game here because you want to get to the deal early enough that you have time to go through with it, but too early and you expose yourself to being gazumped. The closer the vendors are to that repossession, the more desperate they will be to sell, and the less chance you'll have of being gazumped.

Even selling their Property at 65-70% below market value is going to be more attractive to them than completely losing their home and having the embarrassment of having their friends and family knowing that they've been repossessed.

This is possibly the best opportunity in the last 15 years or so to buy properties at a large and genuinely discounted rate. In a Property market boom [growth market], finding repossessions is difficult. From 2001-2007 we couldn't really find many that worked well on the numbers.

The market was in a boom time from the average investor/owner-occupier/man down the pub perspective.

Repossessions are one of the best sources of motivated/desperate sellers that you can find. They've probably tried everything they can. They've quite possibly tried to market their Property with estate agents, they may well have had their deals fall through one, 2 or 3 times, they've had multiple letters from the bank [likely ignoring them all], and they're probably in denial about their debt situation.

They haven't got much time left at this point, so dealing with someone who is **trustworthy and who is fast** is very important to them: far more important than price at this stage.

You'll mostly find repossessions through auctions, estate agents and through your own targeted push strategies using print media such as newspapers, Yellow Pages and internet marketing.

Marketing to find pre repossession Property is different to marketing to find other types of motivated seller [divorce, up or down scaling, relocation and so on]. Your marketing has to really **tackle the problem at hand, and offer the solution**.

You can visit your local County Court. There you'll be able to find a hearings list of repossessions. In this list will be people who have a repossession hearing that day. The judge listens to the explanation from a representative of the mortgage lender, stating reasons why they believe the repossession should take place and why they should reclaim the Property back off the homeowner.

The homeowner, if they decide to, can put their case forward, but most of them don't actually end up doing this. The homeowner can stop the repossession from taking place in many ways, most of which they don't know, or they probably wouldn't be in this situation.

They can pay off their arrears so they're no longer in debt. This rarely happens unless they get a Lottery win on the Saturday before. They can also come to some kind of arrangement with the lender by **selling the Property under market value** or setting up a payment system to pay back the arrears.

The key to getting these repossessions is being decisive and acting fast. As soon as you find your lead [seller] you want to be over there like a rat up a drainpipe! You want to be there yesterday afternoon. If they're highly motivated and if there are other professional investors in the market then you may well have competition. You won't have as much in this market as you may have done in previous years, but that doesn't mean we get lazy, does it?!

Once you have made contact and established that the seller is motivated, you need to remember how sensitive the situation is. The British don't like talking about money and debt, so you don't want to do is go in like a bull in a china shop chucking in offers of £50,000 below market value just because **that's what you want.**

You need to **build rapport and trust** with motivated sellers. They are in a vulnerable position, they're on the back foot and you have to jump through hoops to gain their trust.

Important side note: very often people will sell their Property to you even if they have a better offer from somebody else. The reason they'll do that is because they trust you more, they like you more, they believe you more, they believe that you're more likely to be discreet, they believe that you're more honest and that you're more likely to go through with the deal.

Don't underestimate the Law of Liking [Law of reciprocation no. 4]. Very often people will choose you over someone else *simply because they like you more* and get a better 'feeling' from you [trust].

Don't go over in a sharp suit, don't go over with your business head on trying to fire out numbers to confuse people, it doesn't work. If you do fire out numbers and confuse people then as soon as you leave and they've had a chance to think, you'll get a huge case of buyer's remorse. They won't sell the Property to you, they'll sell the Property to someone else, *even if their offer wasn't as good as yours.*

The main motivators you are looking to fulfil are **trust, speed, timing and discretion.**

Take time to get to know the sellers. Use open ended questions conversationally [questions that don't just demand 'yes' and 'no' answers]. Try and open them up a little bit, give them your mobile number and let them know and believe that whatever happens you'll help them out.

Even if we can't help motivated sellers because the numbers don't work for us, we do our utmost to make sure they are helped or given an opportunity to sort get a solution. My Mum [Mark] buys sandwiches from a Lady who works in Sainsbury's who is going through a potential repossession. Her ex-partner left her and ran up £6,000 worth of debts in her name.

That debt has escalated due to interest and charges [she didn't even know for months] and now the loan company is going after her house. My Mum asked if we could help her and I went over to see her. Her situation was very unfortunate, and the banks do not have compassion in these kinds of cases.

We went through all the figures, but there was not enough equity left for us to be able to buy her Property from her. I really wanted to help her though, and have since helped her make contact with Shelter and the Citizens Advice Bureau, where she has a good chance of getting the outcome she needs.

Even if you can't buy a particular Property, you could probably find someone who could because you'll know other investors who may not have the same rules as you. You may have contacts in estate agencies that could help them out. If they believe that you are genuinely going to help them, then they are far more likely to deal with you.

We've dealt with many repossessions and I've [Mark] been in properties talking to people and they've been crying in front of me because they're in such a painful situation. You have to be sensitive to this and I always go out of his way to help the seller regardless of whether we can buy the Property or not. I understand the Law of reciprocation. They may know someone or know someone who knows someone, they might change their mind later on.

A great resolution is to offer the vendors incentives [sweeteners or 'throw-aways] in the deal. Let's be honest, if a seller is faced with debt it's not going to taste too sweet to them to sell their Property at 30% below market value. However if they sell you their Property at 30% below market value and they can then rent it back from you at a more than favourable rent below market average, then they may go for that.

They're still going to be able to live in the Property, they can still feel like they own their Property, and they will be able to pay a much lower rent than what their mortgage and other debts were on a monthly basis.

You can offer to hold the rent and promise not to put it up for 3 or 5 years. This can be very good because you can almost guarantee that your new found tenant, the old owner, will stay in that Property. Renting back to the vendors who've sold you the Property is a great strategy because they still feel ownership of the Property; it`s still their home.

They still want to live in it, they don't want to lose it, they feel grateful that they still have it and they can make very good tenants.
We have many good rent back tenants who regularly do their own maintenance. One lady apologised to us for painting the bedroom and another lady asked us if she could fit a new kitchen!

Er, OK. Go on then!

You can also agree to allow the vendor to buy the Property back from you at a set and agreed price in a given time in the future. That adds more security in the purchase because the vendor feels secure, and doesn't feel that they have totally lost their home.

These kinds of things [known as 'throw-aways' more about them later] can really make a difference, They'll push the vendor over the line from not trusting you to thinking that you are going out of your way to make sure that they don't lose out. Most of the vendors won't end up buying the properties back, you'll still own them and they won't claim these contracts, options or agreements. Many won't really understand them and many more may never be able to afford to do so.

Remember debt is a behavioural issue.

Summary

Pre repossession Property can be very lucrative for you for below market value purchases. Understand the sensitivity of the situation and go out of your way to be as giving and helpful as you can. If you build trust and liking you can very often strike deals that comply with your rules and help people out of debt. You can also offer incentives and throw-aways to make the sale sweeter and more secure for the vendor.

Advanced negotiation

In "The 44 Most Closely Guarded Property Secrets" we went over many negotiation tactics that will certainly make the difference in you getting Property that you want, at the price you want to pay.

In this book we're going to add to those in more detail so you can make that extra £5,000-£20,000 on every Property. You make your money when you buy Property [like we haven't said that before!] not when you sell.

We are about to give you 32 of the most advanced negotiation techniques. They are not force closes or tricks, just proven techniques that work and will get you and your vendor to your desired outcome.

A few things to know about negotiations before you start: there are rules, tactics, techniques, and tools you can use, many of which are taught in these 2 books. You can also be very creative in negotiations. You can almost create your own rules. You can create your own deals.

By giving throwaways to the vendor: things in a deal that you don't need which you can give as an incentive, you can strike many more deals. They should be of high perceived value to the vendor but are usually of low actual value to you. It can be the [apparently] little things that can make the biggest difference. Throw-aways are explained in detail in this section.

You can create individual and unique contracts. Nowadays it's not just about buying a Property. You can have options to buy in the future, you can rent to own; you can do all sorts of things in making, building and creating contracts that make every single deal individual and different.

Be creative, be flexible and always look at how you can create a tantalising offer to the vendor, whilst still keeping to **your price and your rules**.

There are different stages to negotiation which, when put in the right order will click into place, making your deal making skills seamless and effortless.

Most people think that negotiation is about going in playing hardball: 'this is what I want, this is what I'm going to get, and I'm not going to budge.' 99.9% of the time that doesn't work. There's a time and a place to play hardball, and we'll talk about that in this chapter.

Information & authority

The first thing even before you start negotiating is information. **Information is power** and what you do with that information is power. Before you even start negotiating you need to have done all of your relevant due diligence.

This isn't just knowing what the Property is worth, not just going to 3 estate agents and getting their opinion on the market, not just going to 3 letting agents and getting their opinions on the lettings market, not just going on RightMove and finding all the relevant comparables, not just doing your searches on the Land Registry to find out any restrictive covenants, easements or anything else that might be on the Property that would be relevant to you, not just speaking to the neighbours to find out about the area, the amenities, to find out if there's much crime, not just speaking to the vendors and getting to know them.

You get the picture; there's a lot of information you need to get.

Why? Is it really that relevant?

The more information you have, the fewer 'closing techniques' you'll need to do, and the more you'll effortlessly, elegantly and eloquently talk your way through to a win-win situation. And you won`t get buyer's remorse and sales falling through.

We talk about the Law of authority later in the book. It states that people will trust and believe you more if you are in a position of authority. Information gives you authority. It also gives you confidence. It gains you respect. It also gives you *negotiation power* and *perceived power*.

A lot of people think that authority is about being militarian or authoritarian. That couldn't be further from the truth. Forcing people to respect you doesn't work. It's the people who seem genuine, friendly and have rapport with the sellers who actually hold all the authority.
People will not sell anything to people they do not like or respect, that's a fact of sales. If you seem like you have the answer to every question they have, and if they have tried to spin you a few curveballs and told a few porkies, and in the nicest possible way you've let them know that *you know what the truth is* then you will have perceived power. You'll have *authority and respect*.

As we've said before, and this is really important; you don't always get the truth from the vendors right away. You need to be able to *see the truth for what it is* rather than what you're being told. The more information and authority you have, the more you will be able to see the *reality*.

Know and understand how to use the different resources that are available to you; the Land Registry, the things that are available for public order, the things you can get from the council, websites such as Rightmove, Nationwide, Nethouseprices and Upmystreet.

Contacts

The more people you know who can do building surveys for you, who can do searches on the land and find any covenants, solicitors who can find anything that may be relevant [boundaries of land, rights of way], the less problems you'll encounter. The larger your contact base, the better your chance of success.

Questioning

This strategy or technique is understood in a variety of ways. Questioning [probing or interrogating], is a way of gaining and extracting information. We personally prefer it used as a *seamless conversation* where you're asking 'open ended' questions to get the answers you need without seeming like you're digging and probing at sellers, or making them feel like they're under interrogation.

That's not going to build any trust.

A lot of people perceive a negotiation in the wrong way: hardball arguments of testosterone and ego. We believe, based on some quite phenomenal results that you should see it as is a discussion or conversation which leads to 2 sides setting up an agreement and making a deal that works for both parties.

If you cannot negotiate well, then you will become a victim to those who can. For you to be able buy 18-30% below market value Property you need to be able to negotiate very well. The best way that you can do this [the only way that you can become a good negotiator] is to put yourself right in the mind of the other person you're negotiating with [not against]. How [exactly] do they see the world?

See the world through their eyes

The more you can see the world through their eyes: see what they see, hear what they hear, understand what they say to themselves, understand their decision making processes, understand their motivators, their decision making strategies, the more you know about them, the better you will be able to negotiate.

And get bigger discounts.

Through your probing and your effortless conversation, articulated in such a way that you get the information you need, you can gain a clear understanding of the way they work and think. You can clearly identify their drivers, motivators and 'hot buttons.'

Feeding back for verification

Once you have done this then you can feed back to them exactly what they want which will trigger them into making the decision. It is important that you use the exact terminology that they used so that it resonates with them.

'So let me just run that back to you so that I am absolutely clear as to what you want. What you want is to sell your Property in 28 days to someone you trust, like and who will definitely go through with the purchase. Have I got that right?'

It is very unlikely that they will notice what has just happened. You asked them what they want and then you clearly restated it back to them in their own words.

This puts into practice the Law of commitment and consistency [Law of influence no.2].

Think of it like this. If you sat down with someone and just talked about them; had a discussion about what their passions and hobbies are and what they love to do. What the biggest problems are that they have in life that they'd like solving, where they go on holiday, what magazines they read and so on, you'd build up a pretty good profile of that person, wouldn't you?

Do you think when it comes to negotiating with vendors and offering them incentives so you can get the result that you want, it'll be much easier now that you know them well; now that you know what they want?

Throw-aways

When you're negotiating, the throw-aways can make all the difference. The incentives and add-ons to a deal or contract that you can offer can be the difference between a vendor selling to you or going with your competitor [even if you've offered lower].

We see it all the time in the retail and commercial world. Buy a mobile phone and get free minutes. Collect vouchers and get a free compilation CD of Burt Bacharach. Spend £100 on petrol and get a free cinema ticket.

Maybe this works on you, maybe it doesn't, but it works in general in the market place. It utilises the Law of reciprocation and is an incentive to make a decision now.

If their Dogs are the most important things in their life [we've seen this first hand], then allowing them to stay with their Dogs can be the incentive or throwaway that could seal the deal. It is very high value to them: they're going to have problems renting anywhere with dogs. To you, however, this is a very small price to pay for a 30% deal and a long staying tenant. These are real concerns for people. We have done deals on the basis of allowing pets to stay.

If you know that they're impatient or desperate, then striking a deal quickly will work for them. That will be their hot button. You might be able to leverage a good discount for time throwaways and a simultaneous exchange/completion. If you know that they're a conscientious thinker, someone who likes to take their time, then you're never going to rush them into a decision.

Perhaps you could offer to set up an 'option' to buy in the future. Perhaps you could offer a rent to own scheme where they don't have to raise the full deposit and get to pay it over time by paying slightly over market price rent. You could offer them a buy back clause at a pre-agreed price. You could take rent upfront and make a clause that promises not to put the rent up for a given amount of time.

The very best negotiators in the world are masters of slipping into the skin of the person they're negotiating with, to fully understand what they want. Most of us see the world through our own eyes, that's all we can do. But we need to go beyond that to get results beyond what we're already getting.

Offer solutions to problems

If you're able to offer solutions for people then you'll get great deals. We all want our problems solved, [easily and by someone else]. Motivated sellers have some real and serious problems that need solving fast. You could be their only hope.

Leave the seller happy

Even when desperate and selling Property cheaply, sellers are still going to want to get something out of the deal, and to feel like they've won the deal or the negotiation, or to feel like they've got some kind of benefit out of it. If people can't see any benefit in the negotiations then they will never ever enter into a deal with you.

Negotiations will only ever happen and result in a deal when both parties are relatively happy with the outcome. There are lots of cases of buyer's remorse when buying repossessed and below market value Property. It can be that almost 50% of property purchases fall through.

At the time they may have been OK, but if they'd been pushed into a corner or couldn't see any benefits in the deal, and felt like they were losing out, then they're going to wake up the next day in the cold light of day and think again.

They might get offered £1,000 more by someone else. Because you haven't offered them enough incentives or throwaways you're going to get gazumped or they'll pull out.

It happened to us in our early days. We had a few young estate agents finding us deals: the young and hungry lads who wanted the recognition. We arranged a few cracking deals but many of them never went through because of remorse and because we hadn't offered enough to sweeten the fact that they were selling under value. That cost us a lot.

Speed

The quicker you can do the deal once the deal is agreed, the quicker you can sort the contracts out, and get the purchase through, the more likely you are to do the deal and avoid being gazumped.

If you can exchange within a very short period of time [1-4 days] or can simultaneously exchange and complete, then you eliminate the chance of buyer's remorse [they won`t have time]. In the current Property market with things changing very quickly, sales falling through are not uncommon.

Some sellers have very unrealistic expectations of how quickly a Property can go through. Buyers and agents can give them the 'spiel' just to try and get a deal done. Many vendors believe you should be able to buy their house in a week or 2. They don't understand the Property buying process.

'Subject to finance suitable to himself'

Every time you do a deal make sure that it's always 'subject to finance suitable to himself.'

That's legal jargon explaining that the deal will be done, **providing that you can get finance on your terms**.

Many professional investors will use 'subject to finance' when agreeing a deal, which you would think is OK and would cover your back if you can't get finance, but it doesn't. Although unlikely to happen [how's your luck?], the seller, under this 'agreement,' could turn around and offer you finance at an interest rate of 50%, and you would be legally obliged to go through with the deal.

And you don't want that.

We're not solicitors; you should get the advice of a solicitor, but we do know from our experience that every time you do a deal it should be subject to a final decision. Use this as a negotiation tool. Finance is changing all the time in this market. You know, having read our last book, that leaving deals 'on the table' can be a good strategy for getting BMV later down the line. However if the finance has changed since you agreed to leave the offer on the table, you may have to revise your offer, and you don't want your hands legally tied behind your back.

Sign as nominee

When you sign any contract it can be a good idea to sign as a nominee, which enables you to buy that Property in your name *or in any other name or a legal entity.* This can give you more flexibility in this market.

This is a little more advanced and is something else that you need to discuss with your solicitor. Imagine putting in multiple offers in this market, let's say 15. Then, because there aren't many buyers in the market, 10 get accepted. Perhaps you can't afford to buy all 10 properties right now.

As long as you've signed the contract as 'nominee,' then you may be able to 'move' that contract into someone else's name or another investment vehicle. You can also use 'subject to purchaser's approval,' which is terminology that allows you similar flexibility of purchase.

Leave your emotions at home

It's very important to stay completely and utterly unemotional when negotiating. Remain focused on your outcome.

Property purchases have the ability to take over your life. Vendors who've never sold properties before, who've never been in this position very often panic and could phone you 17 times a day if you let them.

We've had various vendors get really angry, agitated or upset because they are undergoing a painful process. You are very often their last port of call. It's very easy to take this on board and end up becoming very stressed and emotional in the process. This will cloud your judgement.

Stay focused on the end result, understand that the problems that the vendors are having are natural, part of the process and their own problems. Much of what is happening they have brought upon themselves. As long as you've done everything you can, like you said you were going to do, you are pleasant and professional and your team is working around you as it should, then there should be no need to bring your emotions into the negotiation.

You will enjoy your deals much more this way and you'll end up getting the desired end results, more often than not.

Sometimes negotiations will break down; that's just the way it is. Don't chase deals because of emotion. You are number and result focused. A lot of people will chase and chase and get really emotional. They'll end up paying too much, and end up doing deals that don't work for them because they don't believe that there are other deals around the corner. There are tens of thousands of deals all over the place every year.

The belief that more deals are out there every day will serve you very well. You get what you focus on; so you'll get more deals. And you won't end up buying Property that you know you shouldn't. It is the Law of discipline from "The 44 Most Closely Guarded Property Secrets."

If you don't do one deal then there will be another one waiting around the corner for you. It may be tempting to chase, especially if you have blood in the deal; you've invested time and money. That temptation cost Adam and Eve dearly! It will cost you too.

Leave the door open

If you don't get your deal at the first time of asking, leave the offer on the table.

You've built a decent relationship with the person you're dealing with. If the price isn't right don't get involved, just tell them that you respect their decisions, you understand, but unfortunately in this instance you can't meet their needs. If things change you'll always be open for a chat. If they want any help they know where to find you.

That will mean a lot to them because they won't experience that from most buyers. Sometimes it's been 6 months or a year later when we've been contacted again by a vendor we've already dealt with. We've done deals at our original asking price, and sometimes even lower.

The vendor may have been dealing with other buyers who were making promises that they couldn't keep. They may have had an unrealistic perception of the asking price, or they may not have been motivated enough the first time around.

Keep your cool

Be cool and poker faced. It gives you an air of authority. That old Chestnut again.

Most negotiation is about **perception and credibility**. Perception is reality, so what they perceive you to be will be what you are in their mind, even if you're not; even if you're something completely different.

You can be the most excitable, emotional, up and down person in the world who, when you've done a deal wants to go out, pull your pants down and run around the streets screaming like a Warthog. We all feel like that sometimes, and it feels great.

Regardless of how you feel, you need to learn the skill of being unemotional and giving out the perception that you don't even really care whether you do this deal or not. The less you appear to be concerned, the better and more professional you will come across to the vendor.

Look like you don't need it

If they believe that you can walk away from the deal at any given moment, and it really doesn't bother you either way, and it's not going to change your life in any way, then you will hold the perceived power. They will then have to bend over backwards to make this deal work.

No one likes a desperate salesman, do they? You know, the one who is surprised, amazed, excited with a bead of sweat on their brow when you buy from them. The more desperate a person is and the more surprised someone seems when they do a deal, the fishier and less credible it looks in the eyes of the vendor.

Image & credibility

Everything about your persona, what you project and your credibility makes a huge, unconscious difference in the mind of the vendor. The clothes you wear, the reputation you have, your time-keeping skills, your punctuality, your manner, your rapport skills, what other people say about you, how many deals you've done before, what the estate agent says about you, what Car you drive, the way you walk; everything.

You are ticking the unconscious credibility factor boxes; the indicators that vendors need to trust you, even though they don't consciously know it.

If you walk like you've bought 50 properties into that house [like you know what you're doing] then you'll have instant credibility.

Maybe you bought this book because you believe in some way that we know what we're talking about with Property. Maybe you saw our articles in major newspapers, maybe you saw Rob on television, maybe you spoke to someone who had invested with us and had good things to say about us. You bought books by 2 people you may not know [and may not have ever met] because of the credibility factors that were built up unconsciously in your mind.

The more of these you can build up, the more likely you are to do deals.

Perception vs. reality

When you're negotiating, this perception of you is called *perceived power*. You want to increase your perceived power; the power your vendor sees that you have. If they *believe* that you've bought 20 or 50 properties in this same way then you will have perceived power in their minds [even if you haven't]. If you are controlling the negotiation you will have perceived power. If you have a team of experts around you who know what they're doing, you will have perceived power.

In Property negotiation *there is no reality; only perception*. Let's use the great example of value again to prove this point. Do you think that the value of a Property you are buying would be valued the same by you as it would the vendor?

What about the estate agent, do you think she would have exactly the same value as you? The letting agent? The surveyor?

It doesn't matter what the reality is, because there is no reality, there is only the perception of you *in the mind of the vendor*. That is their reality, and you have the power to control their reality of you in your favour, by learning what you have in this book.

Perceived power

If you go straight in and say 'give me the Property at 20% below market value I'll pay you cash be-yatch,' you'll look desperate and give the perceived power straight to the vendor. They have the leverage of price to hold you to ransom. Your cards are out. They can play hardball.

It's **you** who needs to hold the perceived power. You can create this power by having **the answer to the vendor's problems**. If you hold the key that gets them out of debt or gets them out of trouble, you have all the perceived power.

Do you have authority and do you come across as genuine? Does the seller truly believe that you will be able to solve this problem for them? If the seller genuinely thinks that you can buy their Property quickly, efficiently and you do what you say, you'll hold the power. You are the hand that can feed them.

If you can do it easily without any stress, making it look like it's a stroll in the park for you, if you can make **the things that they see as difficult seem very easy,** then you will hold the perceived power.

Social proof

Give vendors written or pictorial evidence of the properties that you've bought. If they see that you've got a nice Car and dress well then they'll perceive that you have **authority**. If you turn up in a clapped out B Reg Nova then they might think that there's no way you own 50 properties, even if you love your B Reg Nova and your wealth strategy is modelled on Warren Buffet.

Remember their reality is not your reality or **the reality**.

Use testimonials from people who have bought from you to reiterate all of the things you are talking about. Third party endorsements are far more believable than self-proclamation. Use third party endorsements from estate agents, letting agents, neighbours, friends and other people in business. Someone else singing your praises is more believable than you doing it yourself.

Take your time

It's tempting to go in like a bull in a china shop and attempt to do everything really quickly because the seller is very desperate. You want to help them out and you want to buy fast. You want to be decisive and act quickly once you've **made informed decisions**.

But the more time that someone invests with you, **the more blood they'll have in a deal**. Instead of trying to strike the deal in one meeting, try to break it down into 2 or 3 meetings. If you can have multiple phone calls instead of one then the **perception** in the seller's mind will be that they've invested a lot of time and effort with you to build the relationship.

They'll then find it much harder to walk away from the deal or offer the deal to someone else [who might offer £2,000 more] but who has only spent 5 minutes on the phone. When they feel like they've given a lot out; they've invested a lot of their time and their energy; that gives you more perceived power. They've got more invested in you.

Why do people stay in marriages for years that they're not happy in?

Where did the term 'don't flog a dead Horse' come from?

You're much more likely to treat someone well if they have £100,000 of your money, than if they don't owe you a bean.

Time is one of the great weapons [tools is a better word!] that you can use. If the negotiations have become a bit drawn out and protracted, and they know that you can walk out at any time and it won't make any difference to you, then your perceived power goes through the roof.

Look at the opposite of that. If you've spent 10 minutes saying I'll give you this, I'll give you this, I want this, I want this, I want this, then it's going to be very easy for them to release the Hounds and escort you out of the door because they've had no time invested in you.

You can play little tricks and have some fun if you want. You can cut meetings short by saying you've got another viewing to go to, to increase authority and perceived power. Don't go too over the top with it and don't tell lies because they'll find you out [and all your credibility will be gone]. Credibility can take a lifetime to build and 5 minutes to lose. Be subtle and conversational.

Reverse psychology

You don't need the deal, and they believe it. That is reverse psychology. You could use flattery [a reverse psychology tool], by letting the vendor know that this Property is probably a bit too good for you. You've viewed many more properties that are in bit more of a state, therefore you might not be able to do anything with this one. You are playing on their feelings of importance to gain interest [AIDA].

As soon as someone shows reticence or disinterest, many people naturally want to know more, and may want to persuade them otherwise.

It will make them feel good about the Property that they own even if it is in a bit of a state. You can always follow up and tell them that they can probably sell this through an estate agent in a few months [knowing that they haven't got a few months], then you restate your benefits and your offers [feeding back].

You've come in through the 'side door', you're almost talking to the subconscious rather than the conscious mind, and that's worked for us many times.

Unconscious signals

Part of the questioning process [your eloquent conversational skills] is not just finding out what they say, they'll very often tell porkies [especially if they don't immediately trust you], it is to pick up on the signals that they give you unconsciously.

Trust your ability to pick up on these things. You know them and you don't need us to write you a body language manual. You know when you're child is lying, you know when someone is nervous, you know when someone is hiding something [stories don`t add up, tapping feet, scratching their nose, buying time, eye movements and so on].

And remember this: while you're looking at the vendor, thinking about what they're saying, what they're not saying, their body language, the way they behave, their reputation, their credibility, their image, they're also looking for all of those things in you.

Like you're long lost friends

People just want to feel comfortable and at ease with you. The more relaxed you are, the more you will feel comfortable [and at ease], the more your vendor will feel the same way. We all feel at ease when we're laughing and enjoying ourselves, so roll some of these things into your conversation so they don't feel like they're being probed.

Make them feel better about their situation using social proof. You understand that a lot of people are in the same situation. It is nothing to be ashamed of, there's a lot happening in the market that they can't control, the government make it hard for us. Make is all seem like it's not their fault and there is nothing they could have done about it.

Make them feel normal and human.

Come across as genuine and genuinely concerned. If you don't come across as genuine or genuinely concerned they're going to see it in your language and all your credibility will be quashed.

Open questions

When you question people, just asking questions that trigger 'yes' or 'no' responses won't find you the information you need. It's very easy to kid people or tell a few porkies by saying 'yes' or 'no,' and it's easy to hide the truth in your body language.

If you use open ended questions which encourage them to discuss their situation, then it's much more difficult for them to hide the truth. Keep the conversation moving and flowing. Words and phrases like 'what,' 'where,' 'who,' 'how,' 'when,' 'how specifically,' 'why specifically,' 'could you give me a little bit more detail,' will trigger the conversation to flow and to become more open and detailed.

You're not just looking for information; you're looking for feelings and emotions from people. If they're talking about divorce and they start getting on their knees and crying, then [obviously] you know there's some emotional attachment there. That could increase your perceived power and the chances of them being a motivated seller. If they're really cold and calculating about everything then maybe they're not that bothered about selling their Property to you quickly.

Listening

A key part of this process is listening. The golden rule is to spend one third of your time talking and two thirds of your time listening.
Too many people spend too much time talking and not enough time listening. When you're talking you don't find out anything because all you're doing is spouting out what's in your head which you already know. But when you listen it's amazing the knowledge you'll get [from doing nothing], and it's amazing the honest answers you'll get from people you don't even know. Sometimes you get too much information!

If you just sat and listened to someone for 2 hours they'll give you their whole life story because that's what people do. The best listeners are the ones who use head tilts, they nod and they say 'yes yes', and they *look genuinely interested* in what people are saying. They are the dark

Horses; the ones who extract huge amounts of information without even saying anything.

Most people aren't good listeners and this is where you'll have a huge advantage. You can go into someone's house, sit down with them, pretty much say nothing for 2 hours, leave and they'll say

'I met this guy he was a really nice guy, he was kind and genuine and friendly and I think he could really help me.' You didn't even say anything and they've only known you for 2 hours!

You made them feel **important** by listening to them. We all want to feel important. Most people wouldn't give them the time of day, and you did. That sets you apart and gives you perceived power.

Be enthusiastic

Be enthusiastic about the way they are and what they do. Listening is a great tool you must use, but it doesn't mean you can fall asleep. Be enthusiastic about the way they are and you'll create rapport and synergy.

Find common ground

Be excited about what they're excited about. People are attracted to people who have the same interests and ideas about things. Find a common ground. Get them to talk about their interests and to get excited about it. You want them to associate good feelings with you.

Be radiant

They are far more likely to want to strike a deal with you if you can get them feeling good about themselves. If you are an apathetic dullard, even if you can help them out, they're going to want to jump off the nearest bridge every time they meet or talk to you.

You can do this strategically and intentionally. Anchor good feelings to you and they`ll have more reasons to sell to you [Laws of liking]. We all love people who are radiant. You don't have to be like Tony Robbins, just give energy rather than suck it out of them.

You know what we mean here, don't you? There are 'radiators' who you meet; people who make you feel good every time you speak to them. People with buzz, energy and charisma who are always smiling and larger than life.

And there are 'drains'. Energy thieves. People who make you feel like you've got M.E.

Once you've built all of these synergies, positive feelings and rapport, it's very easy to slip things in like how much is remaining on your mortgage and the questions that you need the answers to; they'll be happy to share with you.

Use analogies

Whenever you talk, analogies and stories are the greatest tool for getting desired results. You'll see many analogies in our seminars, open days and in our books.

Whenever you're talking, instead of saying everything in first person [me, me, me, I did this, I'm this] talk in stories, analogies and examples. Remember that third party endorsements always increase credibility.

Tell stories of 'when I was helping this seller through a divorce,' and 'when I was helping this vendor out of debt.' 'When this person had a problem this is the solution that I gave them and now they're happier than ever.' You'll also increase your perceived power.

People just aren't interested when you talk about yourself and they'll switch off. Even though it's come from you, it's a story about a third party endorsement. It's a testimonial and it'll bypass people's scepticisms and go straight to the subconscious credibility box ticker in their mind.

Say what you'll do, and then do what you said

You should come across as reliable and efficient. When you say you're going to do something, do it. If you say you'll make them a cup of tea, make them a cup of tea, Don't not make it. If they want the cup of tea strong, make it strong. Don't even give them a chance to question you, because that's what they're looking to do [especially early on] and they don't need much ammunition.

If you say you're going to be there at 3 o'clock, be there at that 3 o'clock. Be consistent [Law of influence no.2]. Be efficient because that's what people want. If they have a certain expectation of you and you're different, they will doubt you.

If Alan Sugar turned up to the set of The Apprentice in a Lada Riva, you'd smell a Rat.

If you've turned up for your first 3 meetings in a suit and shirt with a relaxed collar, in neutral tones, or a smart pair of jeans and a shirt, and then you turn up in your tracksuit bottoms and a Metallica T-shirt, then your credibility is going to reduce and your perceived power will be shot.

Give compliments

Compliment people. Make people feel good. Make people feel important. It's got to be genuine, so find genuine things about this person that you like. What does the seller like or do that you like and have an interest in? It's not hard. Mean it, time it well and it will be well received. It will increase your perceived power.

Be correct & never offend

You must never ever say anything contentious. Racist or non P.C jokes might be hilarious to you but keep them to your friends. You must never offend a seller, you must never argue with them and you must never tell them that what they've done is wrong.

This is the classic mistake that people make in sales and when they're dealing with vendors. 'Your Property's not worth £150,000, it's only worth £120,000.'

Like a bull in a china shop you've gone and bollocksed all the hard work you've done for the last 2 hours. In our last book we taught you the flinch technique. Flinch or say 'ouch' when an agent tells you a price. This is with an agent, not a vendor. People don't like to be shown to be wrong. Even if you are right, and you get them to agree with you [they won't], they will feel resentment and you will have lost them.

First meet them where they are, then...

If you don't agree with them, first you have to come from a place of agreement and then take them from where they are to where you want them to be.

So if they believe their house is worth £150,000 *don't disagree with them*. Say that you understand why they believe their house is worth £150,000, and in the last 3 deals we've done on this particular street, we've ended up buying the Property at £120,000. Never once have you made them feel inadequate or stupid.

Initially you have to meet them where they're at, before you can move their expectations. People don't like to be told that they're wrong. They can hold universal beliefs and identities around being right. Their whole value system may be based on that, and it might trigger their feeling of importance. If you undermine someones feeling of importance then you'll completely loose your rapport and you'll never get it back. Credibility dead and buried.

Summary

Negotiation is not about techniques that back people into a corner and leave them feeling cheated. Use your relationship skills to meet the vendor where they are, offer incentives and throw-aways and look to strike deals where both parties benefit. The more you see the world from the vendors' point of view, the more you will be able to offer them what they want; and get what you want.

Section 6: Accidental to professional investor

The 5 stages for the property investor

Stage 1: the accidental investor

This may be you, someone you know, one of your friends or your family members. This is a common place for people to start investing in the Property market and they don't even know it [which is why it's called accidental].

Anyone who owns a house to live in; an owner-occupier, a first time buyer, someone who's bought a Property that isn't for investment or rental purposes, is an accidental investor. They will make money in that Property year on year through growth, whether they like it or not, whether they intended to or not.

So let's take a £100,000 Property that was bought 5 years ago. That Property could be worth £200,000 now. If you don't believe that, come to one of our Property open days and listen to us ask the audience to tell us how much they have made accidentally. Every time we do it we're amazed at **how much money people have made**. Some people's properties have tripled in value in 8-10 years!

If you would like to meet us personally and see us at one of our events you can log on to this page now:

www.progressiveproperty.co.uk/open-day-offer

Let's go on a safer bet; it might be worth £150,000. The growth of £50,000 in 5 years has been accidental. There was no strategy set up for it; it's completely passive. Some people don't even know they've made that money and they don't know what they can do with that money!

Think about it for a minute. What if you just had 5 of those 'accidental money boxes' now? In no other investment vehicle can you **make money consistently year on year by total accident** like you can in Property.

Stage 2: the cash investor

The cash investor now understands that they have made money in Property over time through accidental growth. They are now aware of this, and because of this heightened awareness they understand that if you make money with one Property [let's say £50,000-£100,000 in 10 years on a £100,000 Property] then with 5, 10 or 20 properties you'd make the same amount on each Property as you did on your first.

That makes reasonable sense, doesn't it?

So what the cash investor will do is remortgage their existing residential Property that they live in, or they'll use redundancy money, or money they've got from selling businesses, or extra income or a divorce settlement, and buy more properties for cash.

They'll believe that's the way you do it. Maybe they have the mindset that they don't want to borrow extra money and they want to play it safe. The may be scared of debt. Maybe they don't understand the concept of leverage fully just yet; one step at a time. They'll buy 5 properties that will cost them £500,000, using the same example, with no mortgages.

That's a good strategy. In 7-10 years those 5 properties will double, and those properties that were £100,000 each might be worth £200,000 each. **Year on year compounded growth** on a £1.2million Property portfolio [original house + 5 investments] could be £50,000-£120,000. They would also make income from the rent [no mortgage] of around £500-£575 per month.

So they've invested £500,000 and got £50,000 in growth and £30,000 [£500 x 12 x 5] in rental income; £80,000 [compounding each year]. That's a 16% return on invested capital [ROCE].

That's pretty good. It's better than a poke in the eye with a sharp stick, [and the stock market **pound for pound**]. It's better than most other investment vehicles. But it's not as good as the mortgaged investor system.

Stage 3: the mortgaged investor

The mortgaged investor understands leverage a little more. They think to themselves:

'Well yes I could get a 16% return on my money, but I've used a hell of a lot of capital, there must be a cheaper way to make the same money without using as much cash.'

A lot of people can't afford £500,000 to buy 5 properties. The mortgaged investor understands that there may be a small risk in getting 5 mortgages but there's also a considerable risk in laying out £500,000 of your own money. They look at investment from a different angle, from a different mindset; they expand their mindset. They think about achieving more with less.

So instead of buying 5 properties for £500,000 cash, they'll buy the 5 properties and mortgage them and just pay the 15-20% deposit on each one [£15,000-£20,000 per Property excluding fees]. They'll raise a mortgage for the other £80,000-£85,000 per Property and then get a tenant to pay their mortgages for them by renting the properties out.

Let's look at the numbers.

The mortgaged investor who could have come straight from an accidental investor and skipped the cash investor stage [didn't have all that cash, understood leverage] has invested £100,000 [£20,000 x 5] to have £500,000 worth of Property. They've invested much less; one fifth of the amount, to get the same amount of Property.

They'll get exactly the same amount of growth as the cash investor would, £50,000 compounding year on year [roughly 10%]. They won't get the same rental income because they have mortgage interest that they have to pay [through the tenant].

Let's assume that there's zero pounds made from the rental income; net cashfow neutral. The total return is £50,000, not £80,000.

Side note of interest: you can cash flow properties as well as get growth [if you're good]. You can also depreciate many things against your Property for tax purposes. Landlords enjoy many incentives for helping the government house tenants [they can't keep up with demand].

Fundamental tip no.4:
You can actually make a pre-tax gain but an after tax loss.

You can claim an after tax loss back against other income and actually get money back for that pre-tax gain! Let us say that again. You can make a pre tax gain, claim general expenses on your Property portfolio, register a loss, and claim that loss back against other income.

For more on tax you can read "The 44 Most Closely Guarded Property Secrets." The mortgaged investor will have the same amount of Property, £500,000 worth, and they'll make £50,000 compounded growth per year that can be **taken as tax free income**.

They've invested £100,000 but they've got growth of £50,000 in year one, so the return on their capital invested [ROCE] is much, much higher. It's up at 50%. If the mortgaged investor had the same amount of money as the cash investor they could buy 5 times the amount of Property and get 5 times the return for the same amount of money. Very good, and if you just stayed on the third stage of the 5 stages of the Property investor, you would make **large amounts of cash consistently over time**.

Our realistic prediction would be that in 5-10 years you'll be financially independent, and you'll have an asset base that works for you passively, once you've set it up. You've let your investment mature and you've got through some of the challenges that you will naturally face.

Stage 4: the leveraged investor

This is where leverage really comes into its own and this is where your *knowledge and skills becomes your biggest asset.* Once you get to this stage it's amazing what you can do.

The leveraged investor will have become so good at buying Property that they'll be able to buy Property cheaply enough so that instead of using 5 deposits to buy 5 properties at £100,000, they can buy 5 properties at £100,000 with one deposit pot.

Their skill will be in buying at such a discount that they can remortgage instantly and get that discounted amount of money [the deposit] back out of the Property. This gives the leveraged investors a Property that's been bought with no money.

Important side note: at this stage we are not accounting for fees to purchase properties. A good leveraged investor will get a good enough discount that they can get the deposit back out and all they have 'left in' or spent to buy the properties are the fees. The 'professional' and skilful leveraged investor will get an even bigger discount so that they can pull the deposit back out, and the fees, and sometimes even *extra cash on top*.

The skilful leveraged investor will be able to buy at 20-30% discount, put their deposit of 15/20% in and borrow the remaining 85/80% [dependent on finance options available]. Then they'll be then able to instantly remortgage to the higher value [actual value not the original discounted level].

For example, a Property has been bought for £100,000 but it's actually worth £135,000. You get an initial mortgage of 20% of £100,000 and then you remortgage to 80% of £135,000, therefore you can get your deposit back out. For exact figures go to page 393.

This may take 1-5 years to learn. There's massive leverage in that, so don't you think it is worth a little of your time? If you work out the figures; instead of investing up to £100,000 for £500,000 worth of Property and returning £50,000 per year [50% compounding], you can actually invest £20,000, buy the 5 properties one after the other, rolling the deposit through each one, and get all of your money back at the end.

If you can crack this you've actually got an infinite return on investment [iROI] because you would make £50,000 compounding on **zero capital employed**. Infinite ROI, 100% leverage and 0% risk once all of your money is back.

That's our strategy. Here is an exact example of a recent deal we completed on for an investor of ours:

Location: Rivermill, Ramsey
Purchase price: £50,000
Market value [reval]: £75,000
Refurb cost: £500
Discount: 33%
Rent: £400
Gross yield: 9.5%
Total money to acquire: £14,850
Revaluation balance: £19,374
Cash surplus: £4,524

Another important side note: there are some key things to remember, and these are the details that will make the difference when building your Property Portfolio. You may be led to believe that if you can get a 15/20% deposit you can get all of your money back in and your money back out. You know that's not true because there are always the fees associated with buying every single Property. Those fees are going up at the moment and there are always lots of little ones [closing fees, telegraphic transfer fees, valuations, legal fees, admin fees] that build up to quite a lot of money.

The actual cost of acquisition will be closer to £25,000 [deposit + fees]. We use a £30,000 [16%] deposit pot at Progressive to account for all fees, contingencies and unexpected costs.

If you've only got 15% discount, when you remortgage you're only going to be able to get 15% back. You may need as much as 24% discount to get all your money back. This is fine in the first 3 stages, but at this stage, by the time you get to Property 2, 3 or 4, you'll run out of deposit monies and you'll need to put more money in.

The rule of thumb: in a growing market where you can get 85% lending, if you get an 18% discount then all of your deposit plus fees should come back to you. In a falling market such as the current 2008 market, you may need as much as 22-24% to get all of your money back, depending on the cost of finance [80% loan to value]. You want to be looking at minimum 22% discount in this market to get you to infinite ROI, 100% leverage and 0% risk. See the figures on page 393.

You don't get that in the bank, you don't get that by putting red Lobsters [£50 notes] under the mattress and you don't get that on the stock market.

Stage 5: hands free investor

Then we move onto the fifth stage for the Property investor. This stage is the one that utilises the most amount of leverage. The fourth stage is great [it's what we do all day every day and we love the results we get] but a lot of people will never get to the fourth stage. 95-99% of people will never get to stage 4 because it takes too much work, too much time, too much effort, too much specialist knowledge, it costs money to make mistakes, and you have to buy a few before you know how it all works.

So the problem for a lot of people is although they can leverage financially, they're not leveraged in terms of their own time. You may not want to be a full time Property investor yourself. You may start out wanting to be a full time Property investor, but you might change your mind for 101 different reasons.

You may not want to do refurbs, you may not want to do remortgages, you may not want to deal with solicitors, brokers and surveyors, you may not have the passion for Property that we do.

The people who understand the benefits of Property investment: the long term cash flow and the creation of your life of choice, but do not have that particular passion for Property, may not want to use up all their time learning the process [that could take them a very long time].

Just like Lyn Smith. View her story here:

www.progressiveproperty.co.uk/lyn-smith

Maybe you're a life coach, maybe you run your own business, and maybe you have your own hobbies that you want to do. You want the *'baby but not the labour pains'*.

That might be you, it might not. It doesn't matter; this book is written for all of you.

Hands free investors *own Property as an outcome*. They invest in Property so that they can have their desired personal life, not so they can be a Property investor at the beck and call of their portfolio. This is where you find someone like Progressive Property who can do the whole process for you.

You pay a small fee and for that fee you get all of the benefits without any of the pain. That's the fully leveraged system where you don't even have to be at ground zero, you don't have to change your lifestyle and you don't have to spend 5 years learning the process.

So what is your strategy? You may want to be a full time Property investor, and if you do you will get massive benefits from this book. Taking just one of the strategies in here could make you £100,000 this year.

You may also decide that having read the book and understanding all the concepts, you want *'the baby and not the labour pains'*. We sincerely hope it's one of the 2 and not the third option, which is to continue to do as most people do; to be one of the Sheep, to be one of the 99%. But of course that's your choice now, and we know better, don't we?

We know what the outside world will never get.

Summary

There are 5 stages to being a Property investor, from accidental to completely hands free and leveraged. The further you go through the stages, learning to leverage more and more as you do, the more cash you will make.

Rules

In the market we're currently in, it is more important than ever to have your own set of very strict rules for buying Property.

A generic set of rules for buying Property might be something like this to get you started:

-Anything under £125,000 [save on stamp duty]
-In your local patch [within a 16 mile radius]
-In 5 given districts of town
-Minimum of 18% discount
-Minimum gross yield of 7%
-No new build, overseas, or off plan
-2 bed, 3 bed houses, studios, 1 & 2 bed flats

That would be a good set of rules to start. Most people who buy a Property don't even have a set of rules that are to that level of detail [and they are very basic].

There are far more things to consider than the list above [for illustrative purposes only]. Ultimately, what your set of rules will enable you to do is buy Property over and over again like Arnold Schwarzenegger.

Like a machine.

Completely devoid of emotion and human error.

Totally *driven towards making profit*.

You've seen the TV shows, what a Dog's dinner they make of it all the time. Why? No rules. The more stringent your set of rules are, the more money you will make. It is directly proportionate. In the early days we used to think that having a set of rules used to rid us of all other opportunities, and closed the door to other ventures that could make money.

'If we can get a bungalow at 18% discount then we'll buy it.'

Who wouldn't when they first start out? Sounds good doesn't it?

We did buy a bungalow at 18% discount. The yield was quite low [the rental return was very low compared to the mortgage payments]. The refurb cost was almost £10,000 more than we anticipated, and in the end we ended up buying what's proverbially known in our office as a kipper.

We were outside our general strategy and at the time we didn't realise it, but outside of our set of rules. It is these kind of experiences that should kick start you into getting your rules as detailed as you can, and *constantly improving them.*

In the end we got most of our money back and we came out unscathed. That was the only Property we had to sell. Buying outside your set of rules won't do you any favours and won't actually keep you open to opportunities. The opportunities you want to make money are all within your set of rules [80/20], the others are the darts that miss the board every time.

Your rules will start in reasonably simple fashion. Like the list we've just given you. As you go on over time they will get more and more focused.

You will end up duplicating, repeating, and systemising your 'Portfolio Building Machine.'

Churning out like a sausage machine: profitable Property after Property after Property year after year after year.

You will find the moneyboxes. You will find the properties that make money and you'll buy more and more. You'll buy street after street after street and you'll forget everything else, because that's what you've *witnessed and experienced that works.*

You want to find what works and milk it and milk it and milk it until such time as it stops working [which it probably never will].

There are many things to consider when setting your rules. You'll want to consider all of the costs of buying a Property. We have a deal analyser that we've built within our business; it's the confidential information of our business. We've been offered £1,000's for this one piece of software, but we've never to this day sold it. It's been touted as the '£4m buying machine.'

This buying analyser has around 5 years of Property buying experience in it; the Property data of having bought around 200 properties for ourselves and for investors. It has all of the experience and all of the costs that we've ever encountered, as an average over those 5 years, factored in.

If we want to make a cashflow analysis of a Property we need to know the gross income through rent, and then all of the outgoing costs. Most people will just put the mortgage against that. Some may be intelligent enough to put voids in and they may even factor a little bit of maintenance in too.

You need to put in far more detail; as much as you can. You need to factor in gas and boiler safety checks and bad debt for potential loss of rental income through tenants not paying [as an average]. It doesn't happen very often, but it happens. The longer you invest, the more reliable your data becomes [that's why 5 years personal experience gives us reliable data: we've seen a lot in that time].

The bad debt, as an average, through your portfolio on a yearly basis, could be £20 a month. That could be the difference between shortfall and cash flow.

You'll also need to know any insurance that needs to be taken against the Property, though it won't always be applicable. You need to know what your average maintenance costs are. You can't guess this, but how do you accrue that data if you don't have 5 or 10 years experience? We always start on the heavy side [think a little pessimistically] and as you go through you will learn exactly what that figure works out to be.

We have put a table at the back for you that you should find very useful, on page 394.

Remember to 'benchmark' and ask professional investors to help you.

Roughly one in 30 boilers go wrong every 2-3 years in our portfolio; that has to be factored in. That's around £2,000 divided by 30 [properties], divided by 2-3 [years].

Of course every Property looks good after a refurb, but after 3-5 years it might need another refurb. The Property might need another lick of paint and a good ol' clean. All of these costs applicable to your portfolio need to be factored in on your own personal deal analyser *before you buy the Property*. Cash flow is the most important part of buying Property right now.

Those who are fooled [not you] into thinking cash flow is just rent vs. mortgage [which obviously you're not], who haven't taken into account all of these other costs, are really going to struggle, especially in today's market.

In our deal analyser we have fields that allow you to put in the mortgage rates at the time. The difference between a 5.5% rate of interest and a 6.5% rate of interest can be £1,000 a year on a £100,000 Property. That's £80 per month; that's a lot of money and it could be the difference between cash flowing Property and shortfalling Property.

When you buy your own Property there are a lot of associated costs, many of which most people don't know until they've bought a few. This can be a real kick in the privates if you're not ready for it. You've got solicitors fees, conveyancing, and legal fees, you've got all sorts of small fees; admin fees here and there, you have arrangement fees that go on your mortgage and broker's fees.

Once all of these costs have been factored in you can make informed cash flow decisions before you buy a Property. A 15% discounted Property can soon turn into a 10% discounted Property when you put in all of these costs.

That wouldn't work on the leveraged strategy, would it?

We are turning away some unbelievable deals here in Peterborough at the moment. We have turned away numerous 20% deals that we would have eaten up like the Hungry Hippos a year ago because they no longer work on our deal analyser; using our rules and our strategy [remember it is personal]. Don't get all emotional, fluffy and sad about it, more will come along.

Here is an example of a deal we recently turned away:

Location: Bretton, Peterborough:
Value: £85,000
Purchase Price agreed: £60,000
Refurb Cost: £2,500
Rent: £425
Percentage discount: 30%
Cash surplus [cash back]: £400
Gross yield: 8.5%

Despite the great figures, the Property was negatively in cash flow.

Computer says Noooo.

And that's that.

Important side note: get perfect later. If you know all of these now, you're ahead of the game. If you know all of these but you haven't got them in a working spreadsheet, then maybe you want to think about putting them in a working spreadsheet now. That will become your own personal deal analyser.

There will be Arnie clones all over the place.

If you don't know these make sure you see them when they happen. Anything that isn't documented will soon vaporise into the ether. If you don't like spreadsheets put them in a word document. Every time you go through your analysis of buying a Property, go through all of those figures and work out if the deal works for you.

It's actually easier to put the data in a spreadsheet because you can lock all the fields in place. You just type in purchase price, expected revaluation, your mortgage costs, your rental income, and it will give you the amount of money that you need as a deposit and the amount of cash flow [or negative cash flow] that you'll get per year.

We go into all sorts of detail in our buying analyser with revaluation figures. How much cash out we'll get from Property, if there's a shortfall, how many years that cash out will pay the shortfall and so on. These are all very important, and we're continually improving our buying analyser. You will be doing the same thing.

Whatever your strategy, whatever your dream, you can make it work, but you need to have your deal analyser and your set of rules in place. You could [in theory] make cash flow HMO's work in the Caribbean [Never seen it yet though]!

Let's just chunk up a step from the rules of Property for a minute. You'll enjoy this part.

Rob Moore & Mark Homer

A stage before these rules are your dreams, your goals, your vision and your reasons why. What's the point of it all? You can have all of these really technical spreadsheets and fancy analytical data around buying a Property. You can have analysis over different valuations and different purchase prices and different rental incomes, but if you don't even know why you're doing it, then it won't last very long.

Is it passion and enjoyment or leverage and hands free? What are your goals? If your goal is to buy 20 properties per year for the next 5 years, and you have a fair amount of cash, then your deal analyser may be a little bit more 'lenient' for you. It might be difficult for you to find 20 properties per year at 20% below market value. Your rules may be that you want to find 12-15% below market value. Not everyone has to turn away the great deals that our 'Portfolio Building Machine' does at Progressive.

You may know that to find Property 18% below market value you need to view 20 properties a week. Over the 52 weeks that's 1,000 properties, and you know that you'll get 20 [view 1,000, offer on 100, get 20].

If you're really risk averse then your deal analyser needs to be very strict, and you may want to buy at 25% below market value. You might be limited to [only] 4 or 5 in a year, but those 4 or 5 in the year will be the best investments you would ever make, and they'll set up your financial future.

If it's a legacy you want to leave, if you have aspirations to write books, be on TV shows, be a professional golfer or a lady of leisure or whatever, then you'll be able to do that, because your rules will create that for you.

It's very easy to get emotional when buying things. We all know that most of us never really buy anything we need, we buy what we want. We've all been there. I [Rob] didn't need 28 pairs of Paul Smith cuff links, 5 TV's [3 of which were Bang & Olufsen], 8 Victor Victoria suits [from black to grey], but before I understood investing, I wanted them.

Idiot, I know.

They all got sold on eBay and a year later those liabilities helped build a £multimillion Property portfolio.

It might seem crazy to buy a Property investment for rental purposes to create income because we want it, but of course we want it. Look at all the Property TV shows: Property Ladder and Homes Under the Hammer; everyone gets so emotional. Once you get emotional your logic and judgement become clouded.

Ladies go into shopping for shoes zone and there's no getting them out of it. Chaps go into German Car mode, and they'll find a thousand ways to justify the £10,000 worth of optional extras they don`t need. They make decisions not based on your deal analyser, but based on some warm fuzzy feelings inside. Warm fuzzy feelings inside don't normally equate to cash, but deal analysers do.

Dehumanise the buying process, take the emotion out of buying; take the human error element out of it. Spreadsheets aren't very emotional. Create a system that a monkey or an unskilled person [not linking the 2 by the way] could use easily.

If you've relied on yourself and no one else and all the confidential information [strategy, rules and deal analyser] is in your head, then you're in a full time job. You may have given up a full time job to be a Property investor, and now you're in another full time job that is just as painful. It's all glorious and exciting at first; the dreams and the vision and the marketing and the sun and the flowing blonde hair on the beaches...

Wait a minute! When you've got 5 properties going through and you've got vendors screaming at you and you've got solicitors who aren't chasing up the work as they should be and you've got estate agents going nuts pulling their hair out...

It's just another day at another office in another job, isn't it?!

We didn't get into Property for that. Screw that Circus behaviour. The more automated you make your processes, the more you can leverage to other people. We'll talk about systems in a little bit more detail later. This deal analyser [your set of rules] should be so strict, so clear and so well documented that someone else could come in and *do a lot of the work for you*.

If they're unskilled you can pay them £12,000-£18,000 per year as opposed to £100,000 per year. You can make that in one Property deal.

Once you're at that stage then you really can create your life of choice because you are not tied down. You're not in Property to be weighed down, tied up and gagged. The investor we know well who lost his whole portfolio broke many of the rules. I remember talking to him afterwards and he had this aura of defeat and didn't believe that Property worked anymore, because it was too much pain, too much grief and too much work.

What can you learn from that?

Summary

Your rules are your strict, unemotional requirements for buying Property that you religiously stick to that make you into a 'Portfolio Building Machine.' Get perfect later, your rules will develop and refine over time. Rules take the human error element out of buying Property.

Systems

This takes your buying rules to the next level. Your rules work best [of course] when you stick to them, document them and take your emotion away. The next stage in that process is creating the systems that enable you to automate your rules.

This will enable you to take one step back. You can leverage and you can be the owner of a business rather than an employee of your own portfolio, which ultimately is the reason why most of us are doing this, isn't it?

Surely most of us don't go into Property because we want to be a full time employee of Property at 60 hours a week because that's what we love. Who really loves that for 40 years? We're doing this because we understand the lifestyle that it can give us; it is a means to a destination.

Look at Mcdonalds: duplicating a process that works over and over and over many hundreds of thousands of times, where unskilled people can do the required jobs because the systems are so clear, and so well documented and rigorously tested to work.

That's when you go from being an accidental investor, to a mortgaged investor to a leveraged investor to a cash investor to a completely hands free leveraged fully Property investor who has to work minimal hours a month just like Tom Ferris, and still gets all the benefits of their whole portfolio and huge amounts of cash.

This is something that will grow with you and will become more and more refined, detailed and disciplined. Get perfect later. Don't outsource and leverage just because you are lazy, and don't do everything yourself just because you're stubborn!

Everything you do in your business should be documented somewhere. Property is a business, in case you hadn't worked that one out already. It's not a hobby, it's a business. You're in this to make profit. There are Laws of business. If you systemise your business and everything you do is documented, you can take a 3 week holiday in Marbella and leave any one person in charge of your business with simple instructions.

The value in our business is in the knowledge that we have in our heads. This is something that we've built over a period of years and spent nearly £700,000 on [in investments and education]. A lot of investors are entrusting us with their money and it's us they're buying into.

But of course if all of the information stayed in our heads and we both decided we wanted to go on a 2 week holiday, then our business would be on standby for 2 weeks. If we had 10 completions going through then they would all fall through. Our business would be completely and utterly dependent on us to the point where it wouldn't work if we weren't there.

That's not a saleable, viable or valuable business. We realised this in 2005/6, and since then we've documented and systemised everything we do, from opening the office in the morning to where all the files are located to how we greet a client. We have a viewing checklist which has about 60 different fields in which we could give to an unskilled worker and, as long as they could read, write and see, they could walk into a Property and ask a list of questions. They could tick off a yes or a no 60 times and we could make a buying decision based on that. We wouldn't even need to be there or look at the Property.

The viewing checklist can then be put into the deal analyser which has 5 years of our knowledge in it. The deal analyser will spit out a 'computer says yes' or a 'computer says no.' 'Buy' or 'Don't buy.' We are following tested processes and procedures that get results.

We started very simply. Everything we used to do was written down in bullet points in a word document. That's a good enough system, because anyone can open a word document and can read a bullet point system and follow those bullet points.

We've become a little bit more elaborate now. A lot of our systems are detailed on flow chart software and we regularly use Camtasia to record a process or task to give audio, video, screen capture and interactive training for users.

These are great training aids, they're not for show, they're a great use of time because if Mark wants to fly away for 8 weeks and Rob wants to fly away for 12 weeks, we're still making money and our investors are still making money.

Systemisation is something that I [Rob] used to think was so boring and so mechanical and so cold. You'll **never sell or have value in a business without proper systemisation**. Most people go wrong because they build a business over 5 years and then they try to systemise it when they want out and have had enough. Of course it's one great big mess and it's a 3 year job to systemise a business from scratch. It will cost you £1,000's or £100,000's, and most small businesses aren't going to sell for much more than that.

Do it now as an ongoing task, starting small, keeping it simple, getting perfect later but documenting everything. In 2 or 3 years time, when you have 10 or 20 properties, your life will be so much easier and you'll be so glad you did it.

And you'll be making much more cash whilst sunbathing on your beach!

Summary

Systems are the backbone of all scaleable businesses and portfolios. If you want to use leverage and have a portfolio that works for you, you will need systems in place to manage all of your processes and procedures around your Property portfolio and business. Own your portfolio and your life, don't let it become another full time J.O.B.

Building relationships [7 steps removed]

In the "44 Most Closely Guarded Property Secrets" we spend quite a lot of time talking about your ability to build relationships with people to get people to like you; to influence people in a positive way and ultimately to *get what you want from your Property investment career.*

We're going to build on what you've already learned from our first book. In this book we're going to talk predominantly about building your team. In 'Think and Grow Rich' by Napoleon Hill he calls it the 'mastermind alliance.' The team of people around you who you can leverage that will enable you to achieve infinitely more than you would be able to achieve on your own.

You probably know this already, but you will not be able to succeed on your own in building a large and profitable Property portfolio, becoming financially independent, leveraging and getting maximum return from minimum effort.

Every seller needs a buyer, every landlord needs a tenant, every person in business relies on a customer of some variety. Everyone is intrinsically linked to another human being in one form or another and co-dependent. Man needs woman. Tarzan needs Jane.

This is what a lot of people forget. A lot of people in small businesses have the 'I'm the only one who can do it' mentality, 'if I don't do it no one's going to do it; no one can do it as good as me.'

If we stay in that mindset then we're going to get to full capacity very quickly [or learn to be a fully qualified broker, solicitor, conveyance, PA, admin assistant, Property sourcer and Property buyer all at once].

We're going to be exchanging more time for not a proportionate amount of money and it's likely that we'll end up in some kind of casket or nuthouse!

The team of people you want to build around you are people who can help you do the things you can't do, you don't want to do, you are not an expert in, but they are. Anything that saves you time and uses leverage.

You will definitely need the help and expertise of surveyors, solicitors, you need to have land searches using conveyancers, you need letting agents to find you tenants, you need estate agents; all of whom have specialist skill sets which would take years to learn yourself.

We all know that it's best to become good at one particular thing, don't we? The better you become at one particular field, the more you can *monetise that skill* and leave everything else to other experts. It is far better on your time. The best in any business, using 80/20, attract the most amount of money.

Your ability to empower people, to motivate people and influence people will determine your results in building relationships, and the amount of money you make.

Fundamental tip no.5:
The size of your portfolio will be directly proportionate to the team of people that you have around you and how good they are in their particular areas of skill.

As an introduction to building your mastermind alliance, we would suggest that you want to look at building relationships with the following people [at the very least]:

Local estate agents

The more local estate agents you know who you build relationships with who like you and trust you, the more properties you will find.

In business there's the acronym RCT, which stands for rapport, credibility and trust. They're the 3 factors that you're always looking to tick in people's minds. Once you have rapport with people so they genuinely like you and feel comfortable around you, your results will start to increase. Once they believe you are who you say you are, you're as good as you say you are, you're going to complete on properties when you say you will, you do have a portfolio and you are a serious player, then you will have credibility in their minds.

Do they like you? Do they trust you? Do they believe you? You're looking to build these 3 factors in people's minds when they think about you.

The more estate agents you have on side who you've built rapport credibility and trust with, the more deals that are likely to come your way. If you imagine that you try and strike deals with 20 agents and only one of them likes you or believes you, then that's one agent who might find you deals. If you've got 20 out there who all like you and trust you, they may not all pass you deals straight away, but of course 20 people is better than one.

The time you spend building relationships with agents is going to bring rewards for you. Estate agents are the best source of deals for us because we've been building relationships with them for 5 years. We have 20–40 estate agents at any one time who, when they sell properties, will think of us. We have RCT and top of mind awareness.

Now is definitely the best time to build relationships with estate agents. They are struggling for business, not many houses are selling and they are desperate for people like you who want to buy. Take your opportunity now.

Letting agents

If you need to let a Property, you need a letting agent. You can try to let your properties yourself but you won't end up being a Property investor, you won't end being an entrepreneur, you won't end up being a business person; you'll end up being a letting agent!

Do you have 5 or 10 years experience in that area and is that a particular area of interest to you? You'll need it if you want to be as good as a letting agent at finding tenants.

The more letting agents that you can leverage the better. You'll find ones who are specialists in DSS [housing benefit/Council paid rent], you'll find ones who are specialists in professional let, some who are specialists in student let, some who are specialists in HMO. The more you know, the more options you have in building your portfolio. Tenants do sometimes default and get into payment arrears, and they do sometimes cause problems. Your relationship with your letting agent will filter down from your letting agent to your tenant, so treat them well, and your tenant is likely to get the same level of treatment.

Building trade

Any builders, electricians, plasterers and anyone who can do handy and dirty work [rich people tend to have soft, clean hands!]. Refurbishing could be a big part of your strategy because you can add value to the Property. If you can spend £1 and get a £3 return, then that's like getting extra discount. You can compound your equity and compound your profit. Refurbs are a big part of our strategy, and our goal is that golden spend £1 get £3 back.

Sometimes it's difficult to find people in the building trade who are really passionate and really committed to their job. There are a lot of people in the building trade who are just happy doing their 8-4 and content earning a regular wage that they don't have to work too many hours for.

In building a portfolio, in turning properties over quickly and refurbishing as quickly as possible to reduce your void cost and to increase your profit, you want to know as many builders as possible. The more people you've got to turn to get the job done, the better. At some point you'll want to upscale and have more than one Property going through [exchange and completion] at any one time.

Relying on yourself to do refurbs, or Derek, [the one man band who has a drinking and gambling addiction and isn't known for his timekeeping], is not going to make you wealthy and it's going to eat all of your time.

Builders and trades people deal with properties every single day. Plasterers, electricians, plumbers; they're in properties every day, they're on the street, they have their ear to the ground and they can be a good source of deals. You might not expect it, but it is important to keep your mind, eyes and ears open.

A good friend of ours, who sourced 28 deals in his last 3 months found 5 of those through referral. That's 18%. Interesting statistic, don't you think. Just by being nice and keeping your eyes open [opportunity] you could get 20% of your deals!

Would you like to know his complete results? I bet you would. His are very different to ours and are very interesting to compare:

Estate agents: 3
Leaflets and postcards: 9
Newspapers: 9
Referrals: 5
Door to door: 1
Joint ventures: 1
Networking events: 1

Surveyors

If you want to get your properties valued at a [market] value that you believe your potential Property to be worth, but you don't have rapport with your surveyor, then their definition of what the market value of a Property might be may be very different from yours. If you're looking to buy, refurb and remortgage to get all your initial capital back, then you need to get Property valued to a higher level. This is a fact: if you get on well with a surveyor then their valuations will be more favourable than if you don't!

Surveyors can be a good source of deals because they go into properties, they're the foot soldiers; they're the people at ground zero viewing properties every single day for a living. An opportunity to those who are open to receiving it.

Mortgage brokers

A potentially phenomenal source of deals. So many people overlook this. In building rapport with mortgage brokers you'll find out what's happening in the mortgage market. They are one of the best sources of information on what is happening with lenders, with banks, in the economy and in the Property market in general.

I [Mark] often have long conversations with the mortgage brokers I use to find out what is really happening every day, in reality, with Property purchases.

Even more simple than that: they are going to help you get mortgages. The more rapport you have with mortgage brokers the more they're likely to be flexible with you and get you finance when other brokers may not be prepared to do so. This is very important when you start out and you encounter challenges for the first time. It is also very important when you **upscale and you need to be more creative.**

And of course a mortgage broker has a database of hundreds [or thousands] of people who have shown an interest in, or have bought, properties. If you're looking for properties, this could be a good source of leads and it could be a good source of finance. There may be people on a mortgage broker's list who have money to spend and money that they want to invest but they don't have the time. You might have the time but not much money, and you may be able to strike up joint venture relationships [JV]. That would be a win/win then!

Posties, delivery boys, people who work in newsagents

They go around delivering everywhere. You'd be surprised how many people postmen and paperboys know. They can be a good source to help you deliver your leaflets, which obviously can equate to deals. Or they may just know somebody.

They hear things, they talk and they're probably a little bit nosy [what else do they have to do?!]. 'I heard the person passed away in this house' or 'they're moving to Australia.' Most people just want people to talk to or to listened to.

These kinds of people are very important to build relationships with. Local people, people who like to gossip, neighbourhood watch members: the people who know what's happening on the street.

Locksmiths, double glazing companies, plumbers

Anyone who repairs or maintains Property will always know someone who knows someone who could be your next motivated seller.

Local Property dealers

All the local Property investors, finders; the people who are getting the deals first; you want them as your friends. We don't often use finders because we are our own finders, but that may not be the case for you [yet], or you may want to leverage more than us.

We know a lot of people who use Property finders; people who take 1-5% of a deal or sell leads to you on an individual or deal basis. If they can make you 18-30% then giving them 2% may be a good price to pay. If they can't find you deals well they'll probably know someone who can.

Solicitors and accountants

They deal with people, they manage money, they deal with legal issues and they're going to be able to tell you of local bankruptcies and probates. They may be able to introduce you to someone who's in a bit of debt, and you might be able to help them out buying their Property very quickly.

Doctors

Doctors have patients who die [really, they do! Remember, you're not a vulture] and there may be an estate you could make an offer on. Doctors speak to people with health issues and they speak to people who may be going into a nursing home in the near future. There may be an opportunity there for you to help them to their desired outcome and benefit yourself.

Local hairdresser, the woman in the sandwich shop, traffic wardens, police officers

The list is endless!

Everyone you meet

The 'third step removed' theory states that if you speak to someone who speaks to someone who speaks to someone; that could be the person who changes your life. You could meet your future wife or husband through a friend of a friend of a friend.

In fact take that process 7 times removed: a friend of a friend of a friend of a friend of a friend of a friend of a friend could extend to the full population of the world!

So once you have gone through 7 steps you could potentially be with people in India or Africa. Most people are very much focused on 'now' and think 'this person can't give me what I want now so I'm not going to waste my time with them.'

But that person might have a brother who has an aunt who might need to sell their Property at 30% below market value. That person might have a brother who has an aunt who is married to Richard Branson, or Richard Branson's cousin.

You never know where your next deal, wife, husband, investor, business partner or best friend is going to come from. Being open minded and being aware of building relationships with everyone is really vital.

You always want to be gathering people's information. You don't want to rely on chance. The more you see people, the more you speak to people, the more you get out there; the more you'll get top of mind awareness. They'll think of you when they think of properties.

This is quite a time intensive strategy but it's something that you want to be doing on a regular basis; getting out there and building foundations. Spend a certain amount of time each week simply seeing people, just talk to people to find out what's going on.

Us English folk are far too often reserved and afraid of self promotion. In Texas people argue and brag over who has lost the most money! You wouldn't find that here, would you? You just hear a little squeak of denial!

A lot of people don't 'promote' themselves because they don't have the confidence or they believe it's not an English way of doing things [you know, we're sceptical and reserved and all that], but it's very important to quickly let people know what you do.

Have a script, an elevator pitch; just one or 2 lines about you that clearly states what you do:

'I buy properties quickly, cheaply, efficiently, discreetly from people who are in times of financial difficulty and I'm building a Property portfolio.'

That's clear. Everyone will immediately know what you do. If everybody you speak to knows what you do then people out on the street will say 'oh yeah I know that lady she buys properties, she might be able to help you or me out'.

It doesn't matter who; people you see in shops, in newsagents, in supermarkets in pubs; the more people you tell, the more mindspace that you will get.

Warning: don't bore the pants off people talking about the details, they don't want to know!

You should always be taking people's business cards and details; their name, address, phone number and email address and you should always be giving your business card out to everyone you meet.

To get **top of mind awareness** it might be that your business card is lying on somebody's desk and they're speaking on the phone and looking at your business card and something just clicks. You never know at what point you will come into their awareness. But if they don't have your business cards or your details then they can't get in touch with you.

Rocket science!

Taking their business card is even more important than giving them out. In 3 years, if everyone you speak to has given you a business card, you could have 5-20,000 names on a the database that you can contact whenever you want. They're people you can potentially market products or services to in the future. There are up to 20,000 people out there who are one phone call away who could help you to your desired outcomes.

Use the concept of **word of mouth marketing** to attract to you all the contacts that you want.

Gossip

You need to tap into the pipeline. You need to put your ear to the ground and listen to what people say. If you ask them questions they'll tell you everything. It's amazing how people love to talk, and you need to tap into that.

No one ever made £1,000,000 sitting in a cardboard box their whole life.

No one ever built a Property portfolio of £5,000,000+ doing all the work on their own: legal work, conveyancing, sourcing, finding tenants, dealing with management and maintenance and so on, without the help of anybody else.

Networking

Your ability to strike up relationships with people who are going to be able to teach you buying strategies, finance, instant remortgaging or bridging facilities, new ways of creating finance quickly, efficiently and cheaply to enable you to buy Property and turn it around quickly, is vital to your success.

We've met many good friends, great long term business associates and partners at networking events, Property events, Property forums, in auction rooms, at business forums and at seminars.

We [Mark & Rob] met at a networking presentation.

Regularly attend Property networking events because you'll learn new things, you'll teach people new things, you'll be able to make Property connections, you'll meet new mortgage brokers, new financial advisors, conveyancers, surveyors, Property finders, business angels, people with cash but no time; you may even meet future partners.

If you are time rich but cash poor then there's a very good chance that you'll meet people who are cash rich but time poor. We've seen this happen time and time again at events we've attended. You'll be able to strike joint venture alliances.

Conversely, if you are cash rich and time poor you will find people who are passionately committed and have time to build Property portfolios, but don't have the finances that you do. Meeting them personally will enable you to make a judgement about their viability to work with you; your opportunity to leverage.

Summary

It's like Chinese whispers. Once something has passed through 7 mouths and 7 pairs of ears it should have reached the other side of the world. Use this concept of word of mouth marketing to your advantage and listen to average people who talk; they'll tell you what you want to know or they'll know someone who can.

Influence

In building relationships and in building your Property portfolio, there are ways in which you can get your desired outcomes every single time without fail. People think that getting what you want: persuading people, influencing people or negotiating a deal that's beneficial to both you and the vendor are very often accidental events [or circumstances of blackmail, deception, force or luck].

This isn't true; not in our case. You can bully and bribe but whatever you coax out of people will not last. There are Laws of influence that work on all of us from a deep inherent psychological foundation. We understand the Laws, we can see them at work every day, and even when we're aware of them, they still bloody work on us, every time!

This section is probably the most fundamental section out of all the books that we've written. These principles are universal and exist within the psychology of every single person. If you understand these [and use them], you will absolutely make all the money in the world that you want to make. You will create happiness for yourself and your family; you will build positive, enjoyable relationships with everyone that you meet.

Most people ignore these 'Laws.' Ignore them at your peril. We're about to give you the 6 secrets of influence, the 6 things that guarantee that you will build positive, empowering relationships with everyone you meet. The 6 secrets that enable you to get what you want as well as delivering for other people all that they want.

Get excited now!

Law #1: Reciprocation

The Law of reciprocation states that in order to receive something, first you must give.

This is something that everybody knows. To be honest most people will know all of these Laws of influence, but most don't end up using them [80/20]. So, once again, in order to receive, first you must give.

If you want to buy a Property at 18-30% below market value and build trust with the vendor [essential], first of all you must give them something. It can be anything. On the Internet it would probably be a free report, 'the 13 fundamental things you need to know before you sell your Property,' or '10 ways to sell your Property before you get repossessed.' A free report on the internet will instantly build trust rather than 'you know what I could just take your Property at 30% below market value right now. Sign here or die.'

That doesn't work.

This applies with every person you meet. It can be anything small; give them a smile, give them a gift, buy them a drink, buy them a book, open the door for them, give them a compliment. The smallest things make the biggest difference in someone else's day, or even their life.

Most people in the world are so focused on themselves, their lives and their problems, that they forget about the wants, needs and desires of other people.

We believe that people are inherently good and of course if we all had time and were all relaxed and had shed loads of cash, then we'd do this all the time, wouldn't we?! But that is not reality.

Just making somebody feel good through the Law of reciprocation will make a real difference in your results and your ability to empower people. In an empowered state people will go over, above and beyond what you expect of them. In a negative, sad, depressed, frustrated, and angry state people kill people for nothing, yet we've never ever known anyone to kill or hurt anyone when they're happy.

You give someone something and they may feel that they now owe you something back; they may feel that they are in debt to you. And a lot of people [not everyone], once they feel they are in debt to you, will go to long odds to repay that debt. They will go out of their way to repay that 'emotional' debt.

It makes people feel good to make other people feel good. Try it and see.

The Law of reciprocation also builds trust. If you take take take you'll put up the Great Wall of China in someone and it will reduce their trust in you. For someone to give you something it instantly builds trust. And of course people will go to great lengths when they trust somebody.

Summary

In the words of the big man himself: first give and then you will receive. This Law in universal. This is the best way to build trust. It feels great and people will feel compelled to repay you in kind.

Law #2: Commitment and consistency

People have a desire to be perceived as consistent through their words, beliefs, attitudes and actions.

'Good personal consistency is highly valued by society.'

Consistency is our way of processing and dealing with the multitude of information that is thrown at us every single second of every single day. If we did not process, filter and make simple all the information we get, we would go insane.

'By being consistent with earlier decisions we can reduce the need to process all the relevant information in future similar situations. Instead, one merely needs to recall the earlier decision and respond consistently.'

People can place great ownership, even their whole personal identity, on certain principles. We use the concept of 'being right' in the book as a classic example when dealing with motivated sellers.

If you barge in to a Property and proceed to tell the vendor that their perception of the value of their Property is wrong, you could be telling them *that they are wrong; that everything about them is wrong*, if they place importance on the principle of being right.

This is a huge mistake that many speculative investors make in ignorance. A very bad feeling will be left and your rapport and credibility will have gone with the wind.

You need to understand that many vendors have the desire to be perceived consistently. In this instance, that means that **they must be perceived to be right**, whether you agree or not.

The key to using the principles of commitment and consistency is to hold people to their initial commitment. The more ownership and identity the person holds to that commitment, the better it will work.

'After making a commitment, taking a stand or position, people are more willing to agree to requests that are consistent with their prior commitment.'

Therefore, if a vendor needs to be perceived to be right [most of them do], let them be right. Get commitment upfront in keeping with their beliefs and then feedback that commitment to get them to take action.

This is a **very powerful tool in negotiation**.

For people who love to be right, we tell them. We tell them often in negotiation scenarios:

'Yes you're right about that. Yes I know what you mean and I agree with you. That's a good colour you have chosen for this room. You were right not to list this Property with an estate agent. Your asking price is fair in a growing market. You're right to want to sell it for as much as is realistic. You're doing the right thing looking at ways to sell your Property quickly. You will have made the right decision selling your Property to improve your situation.'

Never once have you disagreed or questioned their beliefs and identity.

You have made them feel right and important, and at the same time you are turning the conversation to the outcome that you want.

The more commitment you can get upfront, the more you can use that as a negotiation tool:

'If we could strike a deal that is right for you, at a price that would suit you and at terms that would be right for you, would you do a deal now?'

That level of commitment is going to be very hard to go back on, because many people will place their whole identity on it. They go back on that, and in their mind they go back on **who they are**.

Once you get a yes, as long as you can fulfil those criteria, you will get a deal almost every time.

'Commitments are most effective when they are active, public, effortful, and viewed as internally motivated and not coerced. Once a stand is taken, there is a natural tendency to behave in ways that are stubbornly consistent with the stand. The drive to be and look consistent constitutes a highly potent tool of social influence, often causing people to act in ways that are clearly contrary to their own best interests.'
Interesting and powerful, don't you think?

People will add new reasons and justifications to support commitments they have made, even if they are not beneficial to them. Ladies, you know what we mean when you justify why you need those shoes. And you don't really need £10,000 of optional extras on the Car that don't add any value, do you chaps?!

The quotes in this section are taken from 'Influence' by Robert Cialdini, Ph.D. The book is fantastic and we recommend you put it in the queue after reading this book.

Summary

Get commitment from people upfront and feed it back to them to get decisions that will be in keeping with people's identity. People have the desire to be perceived as consistent as they think that is what is acceptable in society. Never tell a vendor they are wrong, they may hold universal beliefs and identities about being right.

Law #3: Social proof

Sheep mentality. Herding. Before we do anything, we want to know that others have done it so that we don't make a mistake, look stupid, or do something that will go wrong. It's like we don't really trust ourselves inside and we need to get external verification that something works. We're sceptical buggers in the UK; we want to know that something works. We want someone else to take the risk before we do.

'Social proof is most influential under two conditions:

Uncertainty: when people are unsure and the situation is ambiguous they are more likely to observe the behaviour of others and to accept that behaviour as correct.

Similarity: people are more inclined to follow the lead of others who are similar.'

If you are going to get a vendor to sell their Property to you at your desired price, you will massively increase your chances of doing so using this Law of Influence.

Show them the deals you have done for other people. Give them evidence to make them feel more comfortable selling to you. Show them letters you have received and videos of happy vendors. The more proof you can give, and the more believable your social proof is, the better it will work.

Why does the concept of social proof work from a psychological point of view?

People don't like to feel uncomfortable. People like to feel comfortable and safe, and of course doing something that other people may not have done before [jumping off a cliff into a waterfall, jumping out of an aeroplane, holding a poisonous spider, buying a Property] will take someone out of their comfort zone; discomfort.

People have a fear of the unknown. If they don't know something and don't understand something they very often fear it. Something that's known, understood or that someone else has done before makes people feel *less fearful and more comfortable*.

People fear being ridiculed by others and if you do something that hasn't been done before you put yourself in a position of potential ridicule from other people; the Sheep and the Crabs.

Summary

People are like Sheep and follow what everyone else does. We are much more likely to do something if other people have done it. We feel more comfortable and more confident with external verification. This is a serious tool in your marketing armoury. Use this and watch people gain in confidence and trust with you.

Law #4: Liking

This is a hugely important one; it might even be the biggest! No one ever buys from someone they don't like, no one ever buys anything they don't like, no one spends time with people they don't like, and no one really does anything they don't like [unless they're forced to].

Fundamental tip no.6:

In order for you to get win-win, empowering situations with people, to buy Property at 18-30% below market value and make sustainable, long term cash, you must be a likeable person.

Even the biggest hard-noses are still likeable people, all in all.

This goes with RCT: rapport, credibility and trust. This is quite possibly one of the most important psychological laws in sales, marketing and Property investment. You should go to great lengths to make sure that people like you, they like what you do, they like who you are and they like how you come across.

Many people will often base their decisions not on fact, not on reality, not on evidence, not on statistics [which is obviously very surprising], but on **whether they like you or not**.

On many occasions we have had investors join Progressive who have made their decisions and written out cheques in a matter of hours. That would not be enough time to do all the research that others may want to do, but it has always been enough time for our investors to get to know us, and to like us. That was **the main driver** for them when investing.

Summary

People will never buy from people they don't like and people will rarely deal with people they don't like. This one doesn't take a genius but it can be the difference that makes the difference. Be a nice, friendly, likeable person to deal with and people will be attracted to you.

Law #5: Authority

Credibility in positions of high standing.

Leaders.

People who have authority can move minds. They can move whole nations like Martin Luther King, like Adolf Hitler [a good example because he was a bugger[!] but could still influence people. This Law can sometimes surpass other Laws, like the Law of liking!]. Richard Branson can move whole organisations. He can get people committed and passionate and filter that down a whole organisational chart.

So you should be viewed as a leader, not a follower. You should be viewed as someone who has authority, standing and charisma. Many of the **greatest leaders have charisma.**

How can you project knowledge, wisdom and power? People react most actively to these traits. People will trust you, believe you and follow you.

As we've already stated in this book many times over, people tend to act like Sheep. More people follow than lead. If you can be a person who has authority and charisma and who is a leader, then you will direct and empower many more people to outcomes that work both for them and for you.

Summary

We all feel comfortable dealing with people in positions of authority. Do you have an air of authority about you [perception vs. reality] that will build trust between you and your agents and vendors? How can you project authority? Knowledge, experience and high standing positions in the community all add to your authority, which adds trust and believability to your whole persona.

Law #6: Scarcity

It's funny isn't it, how we work as human beings. Give us an item, or give us the same item when there are 'only 3 left,' and it's amazing how much quicker we will make a buying decision. All of a sudden we're interested! If something is scarce, if something is rare, if something is hard to come by, we're 10 times more likely to want it just because of that fact [the Law of social proof].

If you look at marketing all over the world, you'll see it everywhere. People are advertising limited supply, limited edition, only a certain amount left, only a certain amount of places left, for a short time only, rare and unique. All of these seem to trigger us to make **decisions more quickly** because we believe if we don't make those decisions quickly they will no longer be there. They'll be sold out, never to be found again.

'The scarcity principle holds true for two reasons:

Things difficult to attain are typically more valuable. And the availability of an item or experience can serve as a shortcut clue or cue to its quality.

When something becomes less accessible, the freedom to have it may be lost.'

Psychologically this works because of the fear of loss. We all fear loss; we all fear the thought that we may lose something or miss out on something. None of us want to lose, none of us want to miss out, none of us want to miss the boat, none of us want to be the one who was too late, who was too slow and who woke up from a slumber when everyone else became millionaires!

Why are diamonds so 'valuable?' Think about it for a minute and think how understanding this can help you get commitment from motivated sellers.

Summary

We all want something 10 times more when everyone else wants it and it looks like there won't be any left if we don't rush now! All the big companies do it: Cherry Coke and Cream Eggs. How can you use this Law to make people more compelled to deal with you?

Modelling

In our first book "The 44 Most Closely Guarded Property Secrets" we talked about becoming an expert [quicker than traditional thinking].

In Timothy Ferris's book 'The 4 Hour Work Week,' Tim argues that you only need to know a little bit more than somebody else to be an expert. There are a few steps you can go through to become an expert which don't involve 15 years getting degrees, masters' degrees and doctorates, and 35 years in any one industry.

Because the time in which we all learn and achieve things is different, expert status is very much a perception.

However the more you learn and the more of an expert you become, the more you'll be able to monetise your knowledge both in terms of building a portfolio for yourself, and educating other people.

One of the quickest ways to become an expert in any particular field is to model the successful things that successful people do.

It's not just Property; it's far more strategic than that. You also need to become an expert in business, marketing, Property and managing your own state so that you're empowered, energetic, focused, driven and motivated.

You need to become an expert in time management and leverage. The best way to do these is to model what other experts do. Model [copy, scrape, benchmark] the things that have worked for the successful, that's given them results and made them cash [and learn from the mistakes].

In the NLP world modelling is a strategy that has been proven scientifically to give you results. Modelling can go far deeper than just copying what someone does. You can go into the full psychological profile of someone; how their thought processes work to enable them to come to decisions.

For example, if you wanted to model Richard Branson, then you would understand that fun is very high on his values, and a lot of the business that he does is based around having fun. You'll also realise that he has an intense desire to improve things in industries where companies monopolise or get lazy. He has gone into industries that have been notoriously tough, such as the airline industry, the train industry and the television industry. It would seem that having a challenge drives him.

If you wanted to model someone like Warren Buffett you might look at his psychology and realise that consistency and longevity would probably be pretty high up on his values list. He looks to make money from stocks consistently over time. How could you use those skills in building your portfolio? We have modelled Warren Buffet because we believe that his strategy is the **best strategy for long term wealth**. He has achieved massive long term wealth and this can be carried across to Property.

And it has been proven to work many times over.

Look at Donald Trump and realise that the excitement of risk is very high on his values list. He likes to make big deals.

How would you like to be as a person and as a business person?

When coaching, I [Rob] always hear the same limitations in people:

'I was born like that. It's genetics.'

'I get it from my Mum and Dad. It's their bloody fault I'm like this.'

'You can't change who you are.'

I would beg to differ. That's the story that they tell themselves as to why they can't do something. It's an excuse for mediocrity.

We've all learned from people we admire. We all copied superheroes as a child, we all fantasised about being something or someone.

How do you need to think to be to become rich and successful?

How do the rich and successful think, act and behave?

Whatever you define as your end goal for wealth, happiness and for your Property portfolio, you can be. You can find the people who have what you want, and are what you want to be. Then model them.

The best Property investors that we've met who've got 20-500 properties in their portfolio have used the same successful strategies over and over again. You already know most of them; buying in specific areas, buying specific types of properties, having an attitude to risk that's maybe a little bit more 'go for it' and a little bit more daring than people who don't have the results they want.

We can learn to walk, to ride a bike, to be proactive, to be focused, to be committed and we can learn to have fun. It doesn't matter what happens around us.

Rob Moore & Mark Homer

Fundamental tip no.7:
It's the meaning we place on everything that happens in our lives that determines our feelings and our results.

Business can be fun and making money can be fun. Making money doesn't just enable you to have the life that you want, but the people around you too; your friends and your family to have the life that they want, thanks to you.

Making money doesn't have to be a sin and making money doesn't have to be riddled with guilt. These are all choices. If you model the most successful people in business and Property, there will be many beliefs that they hold that are very similar. You certainly won't find any Property investor or international businessman believing that making money is wrong, or is some kind of crime. They'll love it. And probably give a lot of it back later on in life too.

It's not just Property books that you want to be reading and Property investors that you want to be modelling. You also want to be reading business books and studying businessmen and people in general who have succeeded.

Donald Trump went through many trials and tribulations in his career. He was over $1billion in debt at one point. He realised that it was a lack of focus and a lack of commitment that had got him where he was, and he managed to change his fortunes around. I would suggest reading some of his books.

There are many mentors that we've studied: "How to be a Billionaire" by Martin Fridson is a great book that actually studies the profiles of many of the world's most famous billionaires. It talks about their strategies, their background and the story of their life.

Many of these people are very eccentric and have unbelievable qualities in certain areas [and sometimes they lack in other areas].

Howard Hughes was a billionaire who had some serious OCD issues! J. Paul Getty was renowned for being what you might call 'weird' but made a huge amount of money.

Money doesn't judge.

The more you read about successful people, the more it will drive and motivate you. It will give you focus, momentum and social proof.

We'll let you into a little secret: the same stuff will come up: *faith, desire, passion, commitment, focus, determination*, risk and so on. Napoleon Hill summed them all up in 'Think and Grow Rich' when talking about Henry Ford, Andrew Carnegie and other incredibly successful people.

90% of the game is up in your head, it's not just about the mechanics. We would make it a constant, lifelong mission to develop your personality just like you're developing your knowledge. Model other successful people and *become the person that you want to be*.

Remember; this isn't about trying to be somebody else and this isn't about trying to do things that just aren't you. This is about creating the 'you' that you really want to be. If you aren't confident, and you want to be, what are you going to do about it?

In terms of your personality, you are what your 5 or 10 highest values are. To determine your values; the things in life that you place the most importance on by which you live your life, ask yourself the simple question:

'What is the most important thing for me in the area of Property and business?'

Ask that to yourself 10 times, push yourself through a blank spot or 2 and there you have them; the 10 most important things to you in that particular area.

Once you have done that, and listed them out, go through this book and decide what values you believe you need to for you to become who you want to be.

We have created room at the back of the book for you to do this. Turn to page 395.

Let's talk about money.

95-99% of people put money right down at the bottom of their values list [and they may not even know it]. They'll have limiting beliefs about money and here are just some of them [how many times have we heard these?!]:

'Making money is sinful.'

'Making money is evil.'

'In order to make money you have to take from other people.'

'If you focus on money you're not focusing on love and caring and karma.'

These are all beliefs. They're not real! You could just as easily have the following belief:

'I am going to earn as much money as I can so that I can look after my family and my friends and I can give back to charity when I die.'

Surely that's more empowering than all of the negative and limiting beliefs put together. Just looking at your values list and moving money from number 52 and up to number 3 or 4 will instantly focus you on that much more than you ever have done, and your results will be relative to that.

Maybe you want to move passion up, so that you do things with excitement and energy. Maybe commitment and focus need to be higher, knowing that it works for very successful people. Tony Robbins has so much genuine passion in what he does, how can you not be attracted to that passion?

Summary

The most successful people are so because they have successful traits and characteristics. Some are learned but most are borrowed, copied or modelled, as inspired by heroes and mentors. Think carefully about who you want to be and what you want to achieve and replicate the traits, characteristics and strategies of the successful people who already have what you want. Create the person you want to be and don't be a product of 'your upbringing' or 'your parents.' You have the ultimate choice.

Play [and win] the numbers game

Everything to do with success, making money and building a Property portfolio is a numbers game, when broken down.

Numbers may be your strong point, if so get excited!

Numbers may not be your strong point, if so *learn* to get excited!

For me [Rob] numbers and spreadsheets and accounts and calculations of averages and statistics and analysis were not natural skills. It wasn't something I particularly enjoyed. However Mark on the other hand; it's like riding a bike for him with no hands; a totally natural skill.

I'm going to talk about him now while he's not looking! Don't tell anyone [Sshhh].

All Mark sees is spreadsheets, figures and numbers. I have to admit I found this totally weird at first, but more about that later in the chapter...

The ability to see what a Property looks like in 1's and 0's and digits is *what will make you all the cash*. It enables you to cut through the emotion and see a Property in its true light: a money box or a money box with an unplugged hole in the bottom.

Fundamental tip no.8:
Viewing Property numerically [as opposed to emotionally] has made us a lot of money. Emotion has cost us money.

We're both very different in terms of what is a natural, born or nurtured skill. However I soon realised that I had to learn the skill of thinking in numbers if I was ever going to make any money, and I have Mark to thank for that. Why was I £30,000 in debt? Because I did not *keep my eye on my money*.

I had to make sure that money stopped going out. The first stage of that process was awareness. Once the hole was plugged, money started coming in and stopped going out; very simple. So why didn't I do it all along! I just wasn't watching it closely enough to get a grasp of what was really happening.

...so Mark sees 1's and 0's. He sees buying Cars as a series of numbers: cost of capital, depreciation, wear and tear, cost of servicing, consumables, running costs, 0-60 times and miles per gallon.

He sees girls as numbers [like I said, he's not looking]. How much will she cost me? Can I get a return on my time? Is she an entrepreneur? What is the CPF ratio? [I can't tell you what that means!].

Oh he'd probably kill me if he reads this but I'll slip it through. It will be far too late once you are reading it Mark [Ha!].

But seriously, if you're not number focused [some people don't even open their mail or their bills] then you really won't know where you are. You'll guess and you'll get it wrong and you'll be in denial!

Not you, of course. Them.

Where are you now? The first skill in numbers is knowing exactly where you are to the penny.

Like I said it was a learned skill for me. I have taught myself to really enjoy number crunching and appreciate that the process makes me money. I enjoy making money so I enjoy this process:

Profit and loss statements on our business, cash flow analyses, sensitivity analysis for our Property portfolio and our businesses, the statistics from the marketing we do, the amount of calls we need to get a lead, the amount of leads we need to get to the number of deals we do, the number of properties we view to the number of deals we secure, the number of deals that we secure to the number of actual completions that go through, the hours worked a day that are income generating [IGT] to non-income generating and so on and so on.

Breathe.

You'll understand more the mechanics of what's going on in your Property portfolio; *the reality*. You will be able to identify where you are draining money and plug the holes that leak. You'll be able to ascertain what works and upscale to compound your results and make cash.

Numbers are quite simple. They don't judge and they don't lie.

The reality of a numbers game: you'll throw many darts at a dartboard and some will miss completely. Some will hit the board on the outer ring and some will hit the wire and fly right back at you. Some will land in green, some in red and some [a few] will hit the bullseye.

Leave the ones that missed the board: disregard those; they're no good to you. There will be many marketing strategies that you try for your Property investment portfolio. There'll be some properties that you buy that just don't cut it for you. You could have been convinced that they would make you an absolute packet at the beginning, and they'll end up being the bain of your life.

They're the darts you throw that miss the board. Understand that you'll always miss the board every now and again, and that's all part of the process. More often than not, you'll probably miss the board [80% of the time?].

In fact there will be a lot of things that you do when you start that you wouldn't touch ever again with a bargepole [overseas HMO's off plan in the Caribbean!].

Even years down the line you'll be trailblazing and testing and finding new darts that hit the bullseye, and still more will miss the board. Some will miss by so far you'll think you've thrown it backwards.

It's not a bad thing to try and fail, we don't even believe in the word anyway, so you won't read it again in this book. Keep going, keep trying to improve your results. If you've tried to improve and it still doesn't work, you can tick that one off the list, bin it and not go down that road again. That's one less thing that doesn't work off your list. Go through that process enough times and there won't be many things left that won't work for you!

Property numbers: for every 50 properties you'll be lucky if 10 were good investment propositions. From that 10, you can offer on them all, you could strike deals on 3 [if you're good] but more realistically 2 will go through. Even then one or both could fall out of bed.

So you've done that 50 and you've got whatever results you've got.

When you do the next 50 you won't focus your time on the darts that missed the board, will you?

We don't throw overseas darts, we don't throw off plan darts or new build darts, and we don't throw darts all over the country. Not because of any bias, stereotype or personal agenda, but because those darts have never hit the bullseye for us.

Improving those numbers: the next 50 properties that you view will be just like the 10 that you agreed to do a deal from the last 50 you viewed, won't they? That is 80/20 thinking. That will *make you cash*.

The less time you spend on things that don't generate you money, and the more time you spend on things that do, based on your numbers, will be directly proportionate to the amount of money that you make.

The key things to remember when you're doing your numbers are:

Enjoy the process: when you look through your statistics and data and you can actually pinpoint where you're making money, that's very exciting. Learn to get excited about that process. Some of the best questions that we've ever heard to ask yourself through this process are:

'How can I do this and enjoy the process?'

'How can I call all these cold sales leads and enjoy the process?'

'How can I go through all my numbers and enjoy the process?'

It might seem to some people that getting excited about numbers is like getting excited about watching bowls on BBC2 at 3 o'clock on a Sunday afternoon. Of course to some people bowls at 3 o'clock on a Sunday afternoon is quite exciting.

There are certain skills that you need in every facet of life. If you want to drive you can't ignore the Highway Code. If you want to ride a bike you can't get by without using the brakes.

If you don't like spreadsheets, use a word document. If you don't like computers write in a notebook or a piece of paper, it doesn't matter. As long as you're making a note of the amount of calls you make, the amount of leads you generate, the amount of deals you do and the amount of money you are making and spending [net], then you'll be able to monitor your progress and *measure your results*.

We're not playing pin the tail on the donkey here, you need to know what you're doing to be able to improve what you're doing and if you don't know what you're doing then you can't improve it.

Genius discovery 101!

This is what gets my back up about mass media advertising [Rob]: sales people for major publications, magazines and newspapers will sell you advertising space that you'll have to pay £100's or £1,000's for *without any tested results*.

You could be chucking a load of money down the drain [and do you think they would care?].

Look, I know they are only doing their job like anyone else. But don't you think their ability to sell ad space would go through the roof if they could give us some *real numbers?*

It's not rocket science. As soon you put a unique 0800 number on ads that you are testing then *you have control*; you have data to work from. You know that every person who rings that number has come from a specific ad. Ads can be measured against each other to see which one produces the best results.

You'll know within a couple of weeks what works and what doesn't, without spending a grand to find out. If it doesn't work you bin it.

Remember though: it's not just about trying it once; you might need to try it 10 times until you start hitting the board. You might need to try different headlines, different calls to action and different media publications.

The *most successful Property investors* and money makers in the world aren't so by accident; most of them haven't had a silver spoon in their mouth. What they're consistently good at is leverage. They save 90% of their time by not having to test everything from scratch, because they learn from the experts. They learn from 90% of mistakes that the experts made when they weren't experts.

Once they've based their strategies around those who are successful, rich and have big portfolios, they can test and continually improve on what they do. They are now playing with the final 5-10%; the **difference that makes a difference**.

A great quote that we used in the first books that was one of the fundamental tips was **'get perfect later.'** Don't get too analytical about it all at first. Start jotting your numbers down, making logs and as you do it [the more you do it] you'll get perfect later; for now just get cracking.

It's amazing how much analysis you'll go into later on once you've got results. This is a mistake we've made in the past: you get to the point where you test the smallest of things which make fractions of a percent difference. You can spend a lot of your time for very small improvements.

You know what we're going to say now, don't you?

Use the 80/20 principle. Think about what's going to make the best use of your time, what's going to make the biggest difference, make you the most money and give you the most happiness.

Testing headlines in newspaper or internet ads is a good use of time. However testing whether you capitalise the first word of the paragraph or not may not be such a good use of time. You may need hundreds of thousands of responses to get any true data.

Read about the concepts and details in books. Learn from other successful people to save you time, and do the things that make the biggest difference yourself.

Summary

Property and making money is all about the numbers. Don't be scared of them, they don't bite. Don't over analyse them; you'll still need to take action. Test and measure your marketing results and cash flow and you'll keep making more money. The more you shoot, the more you'll score. The more you offer on, the more you'll buy. Get perfect later, start where you are and then improve your numbers as you go.

Rob Moore & Mark Homer

Section 7: Learn from their mistakes

The 10 most common mistakes to avoid [like the plague]

1. Giving up

In Malcolm Gladwell's book 'The Tipping Point,' he talks about that point at which all the hard work that you've done gets to a tidal wave where everything is just about to start happen for you.
It's at this point, or just before this point, that most people [99%] give up.

People want instant results. People expect [and are marketed to expect] instant results, and if they don't get them, they get bored, stomp their feet, cry like babies, cross their arms in a huff, get sick and tired, and go on to something else.

And then they go through the same cycle all over again.

The reason that 99% of people fail is because they give up. You only fail when you give up; you know that. You only don't finish the race when you stop running. If you keep running you'll finish the race, whether it's a sprint or a marathon. As long as you keep running you'll finish the race.

No shit.

Such a simple concept that we all know. But as soon as things get a little bit tough, most people can't stand the heat, and they leave the kitchen. They're always looking for the easiest, most comfortable solution.

A quick tip: if you're comfortable in everything you're doing you're not getting anywhere. Sometimes you need to be pushed out of your comfort zone, you need a kick in the backside, you need a push; you need to struggle a little.

Jump out of a plane and you'll understand what exhilaration is.

If you consistently continue to grow and develop; you do, rather than just to talk about what to do, then you will become everything that you want to be.

This is by far the biggest mistake people make. We talk to so many people who say:

'Oh I tried Property. I bought one and it didn't work.'

'I remortgaged and bought 5 new build, off plan HMO's in the Caribbean; oh I tried Property it doesn't work.'

'I bought and sold a Property and didn't make me any money.'

We've spoken to hundreds of people who have 'thought about' or have 'tried Property.' Of those hundreds of people less than 5% are still going that we know of. The ones who are still going are making it work and are making money, because they keep moving forward and finding new ways and learning the *necessary lessons*.

All the others haven't and aren't because they gave up, they're not doing it anymore and they're probably not making the money they want to.

Summary

Everyone who gave up failed. No one ever fails until they give up. If you really want something and you never give up, you'll always get there. Be a tough resilient little tyke and you'll get what you want.

2. Thinking small

It's very easy to think within the boundary conditions of our mind, limited by what we believe we can achieve from what we've seen and done.

That's all we know.

The problem with only believing that we can do what we've already done, is that we won't be able to do what we haven't yet done! That's not going to get us very far, is it?!

That's small thinking.

In order for us to become a millionaire we need to think like a millionaire. We need to **think much bigger** than where we are now if we have aspirations to be somewhere bigger and better. Don't be constrained by your own reality right now.

Yes, this is a mind shift for some; a change in thinking. It might be uncomfortable too, but to become a millionaire you've got to **think like a millionaire before you're a millionaire!** You're not going to do that thinking small; like you're on £22,000 per year.

You have to think like you own 10 properties and 20 properties and you have to believe that you are there already. Look at the opportunities to buy 5 instead of one. Look at the opportunities to use other people's money instead of your own. Think big; believe that anything can be achieved.

Anything that you want has already been achieved by someone else, who didn't always have what they've now got. And they had to do the same as you.

Summary

Poor people think small. We are all bound by the limitations we create in our mind, and none of that is reality. Learn to think and dream big because you get what you focus on.

3. Playing too safe

Most people aren't prepared to take a risk.

They've worked hard in their life for what they have and they're not going to blow it by remortgaging their Property and throwing it at a load of other properties! None of the successful Property investors ever built a Property portfolio of 10, 20, 50, 100, 200 or 500 properties by never taking a risk.

Sure; if it's raining you won't get wet if you don't leave the house. But if you never leave the house what are you going to achieve [other than housework]?

There is always a certain amount of risk in investing; we all know that. We know that investments can go up as well as down. But if you don't speculate, if you don't give your money a chance to grow through investing, it never will.

If you leave the money in your home your earning capacity will be limited to that one Property. The equity will be idle. If you remortgage it and reinvest it wisely [taking a little bit of a risk], moving out of your comfort zone just a little; with risk comes reward.

Your attitude to risk will be individual to you. You might be prepared to risk 40 or 50% of your income. You might only be prepared to risk 5 or 10% of your income. The choice and the strategy are down to you as an individual.

Those who play it too safe never experience the fruits, joys or passions of life. Living a flat line existence will never make you happy, let alone rich. Many great millionaires and billionaires have been bankrupt before, but because they've taken risks [that don't have to be huge]. The highs are much greater than the lows.

Summary

Money sat in the bank won't make anyone a millionaire. Never taking a risk may be comfortable, but no one ever achieves anything inside their comfort zone. With risk comes reward. Think about your attitude to risk and what you are prepared to invest. There is a huge difference between investing and gambling, we are not talking about putting all your cash on Eor, the 3 legged horse at the 3:15 at Kempton.

4. Getting too emotional

We used to work for someone who was so emotional that when everything was going well he would run out of his little corner office saying "We're all going to be millionaires this time next year Rodney!"

Everything was fantastic and we'd all be buzzing for 5 minutes, but then of course some little challenge would happen and he'd be on a downer and we'd all be sacked the next day if we didn't go and make 15 sales each.

The problem with that level of emotion is that you can't make logical based decisions. If you make emotional based decisions they'll often be wrong. If you make emotional based decisions around money, finance and investing, you're going to lose money. Think about making logical decisions based on fact, evidence, experience and knowledge; not emotion.

Learn to control your emotions. Yes be excited and be passionate, but when it comes to making investment decisions think about analysis, experience, what you've learned and what you know. Don't negotiate on emotion; that is where most people go wrong. It's easy to get carried away with hype, excitement and marketing, but ultimately is that really what's going to make you money?

Summary

Emotions cost money. Emotions cloud judgement and override logic. Logic makes cash. Keep your emotions in check, leave your 'stuff' at home and stick to your rules and strategies as you set them now in this book, and you'll make cash.

5. Lack of diligence

There's a fine line between doing the right amount of diligence and analysis paralysis. Many people use research as an excuse; they may be doing research for the rest of their life and that's not going to get them anywhere.

Knowledge without action is useless.

Conversely, making investment decisions without any knowledge, experience or research is going to increase your chances of losing money. You're risk becomes lower as your knowledge and experience gets higher. The more knowledge you have of a subject and the more research you've done, the lower the risk, and that's why the **experts make all the money**.

Do your diligence, research and analysis to reduce your risk and make decisive, informed decisions.

For more on diligence for Property investment and the specifics, read "The 44 Most Closely Guarded Property Secrets."

Summary

Pinning the tail on the donkey blindfolded or putting all of your money on red won't make you rich. Understand to the best of your ability what you are getting into, and remember that the increasing of knowledge is directly proportionate to the reduction of risk.

6. Using your own money

No one ever became a millionaire using the million they had sat in the bank. It doesn't work like that.

In order to make a million you've probably come from a point where you didn't have that money. Most multi-millionaires didn't start with multi millions. Sure, some people got fed the silver spoon, but most millionaires are self made.

The key is leverage and using other people's money and time to build wealth.

Most people use their own money [it's all they know]. They'll work and they'll work and they'll work and they'll work and they'll put their money in a bank and they think they're getting interest of 5% but of course that's never going to make them wealthy. Especially when you take off tax and inflation!

Understand leverage; using the bank's money. Leverage the money of financial institutions. Most people cannot understand the concept of using other people's money; therefore their strategies in their mind are seriously limited and they'll be stuck in the same place. They'll be using their own money to invest but they'll also be spending their own money; so their wealth won't go up.

Summary

Millionaires use other people's money to invest. They love leverage and they see it as reduced risk. It will take years to work and save enough cash to have enough to invest and compound, and become financially independent. That is the great attraction of Property over every other investment class.

7. Wasting time

80% of your results are based on 20% of your time input. The converse is also true. If 80% of your results are from 20% of your time, what are you doing with the other 80% of your time? Most people are wasting it.

If we spend the other 80% of the time focusing on the things that get 80% of the results, we can increase our effective earning power by 500%.

Facebook, 3 hour lunches, 3 hours of the day in front of the TV: that's most people's 80%. Yes it's good to have downtime and you have to do the things you enjoy; I love the Apprentice and I love Dragon's Den and I love Ultimate Fighting [Rob] but they're the only 3 TV shows that I watch.

Those shows take up maximum average 1.25 hours per week. Every single minute of every single working hour should be spent, if possible, on things that make you money, dealing with the income generating tasks [IGT's].

You don't have to be obsessed like us about time. Remember you will create far more free time if you use the 80/20 principle and make your time count. You'll find more with less, *you'll earn more with less*, you'll get more with less; you'll be able to do more of what you want to do more of the time.

Timothy Ferriss works 4 hours a week, and still manages to travel around the world chasing his dreams.

Most people do things habitually. They spend 3 hours on their emails in the morning by habit. There's probably only a handful of pressing emails that they have to reply to a day, yet people will spend a third of their day on Outlook [easy, comfortable].

People kid themselves that they are working when they are not, which is why a work log is so important.

The quickest and easiest way to manage your time is to write a small list the night before the next day, with a maximum 5 things, numbered one to 5, of the 5 most important things that you need to do the next day.

Start at number one. Only ever go to number 2 once you've finished number one. Only go to number 3 once you've finished number 2. Some experts in time management might argue that you should only spend time on the 2 most important things of the day and discard everything else.

Don't let your phone rule your life.

About 2 years ago, we were ruled by our phones. You get to a point when you're doing a lot of deals; people are ringing you all the time, you have more and more contacts and it gets really hard to manage your own time. You become a slave to other people; phone, email and circumstance, and it gets really hard to take control of your own time and get anything important done.

Picking up the phone willy-nilly to people will waste your time. You'll be halfway through tasks that you won't remember where you were when you get back to them. You won't finish those important tasks.

Can you ever get hold of rich and successful people on the phone? There's a good reason for that.

How you prioritise your time and how strict you are with your time is very important. How you use your time will be directly proportional to the amount of money that you earn.

Summary

The biggest hole in your money box will be wasted time and energy. How are you using your time, and can you do more with your time that generates you the money? We know that there are so many distractions so just ask yourself: is this the best use of my time and will it take me where I want to be?

8. Lack of flexibility

The market is always changing. The economy is always changing. The environment is always changing. Life is always changing.

As you already know, the market this year is radically different to what it was last year. If you're still doing deals, making negotiations and running finance in the same mindset as you were last year, then chances are that you don't have a business and your Property portfolio is losing money hand over fist [if you still have it].

It's so important to be flexible, now more than ever. We have the advantage of youth; we haven't done the same thing for 50 years, so we're quite flexible. Having that youthful mentality [no matter how old you are] is so important.

Look at Alex Tew of the Million Dollar Homepage and Mark Zuckerberg of Facebook: young entrepreneurs who are clearly flexible and opportunistic. Young businessmen who understood the leverage that could be attained on the internet.

I know people who still can't grasp the internet properly; intelligent and well educated people. Unfortunately these people are going to be left well behind. In 10 years time there'll be something that's bigger and more amazing than the internet. Where will you be? Right up there, we expect.

Finance deals that you're doing this month might not work next month; that's the reality of the market right now. You need to be quick, you need to be flexible, you need to be open to change and you need to accept change. Change is part of growth and development.

Be realistic about change. Find a strategy that works: milk it, work it, roll it out, duplicate it, triplicate it, replicate it and upscale it. Remember, however, that things change and you need to change with it. If things aren't growing they're dying; **nothing ever stays the same.**

Summary

Businesses go bust if they're not flexible. Times are changing so fast more and more, that our ability to adapt and move with the times will have a big impact on the amount of Property we buy and the amount of cash we make. Most people see change as a burden. You can see change as an opportunity. With every new phenomenon [the internet, web 2.0, social networking] more millionaires are made to opportunistic and flexible people.

9. Lack of focus

Look at the majority of people: emails come in, attention is distracted, they read the emails, they check their personal email account, Facebook, MSN and a bit of surfing on the net and before they know it it's 3pm. They're doing 5 tasks at once on 3 computer screens but not actually getting anything done.

We've certainly done that and it isn't productive.

Chasing too many rabbits catches none. Buying all over the place can make you bankrupt [we know people who have experienced this]. Chasing MLM schemes that never work can take all your time and energy for little reward. Looking at the next get rich quick won't get you rich at all. Doing stocks and shares and bonds and euros and Forex all before any one has made real money, won't make you real money.

It's all a lack of focus. The more you spread yourself, the fewer steps forward you take. Laser like focus is the only way to achieve the results you demand for yourself. There's so much marketing noise out there; so much fluff and so many things glisten that demand your attention; all glitzy and shiny. Good luck juggling your knives and firesticks.

The best professional sports people are the ones that can totally clear their mind, visualise and *focus on the one thing that is right in front of them now*. If that is the finish line 100m away, then that is what needs to be focused on. Thinking about the twinge in your foot or the lack of training and preparation doesn't help at that moment.

Golfers and Cricketers know that 100% focus on the next shot is vital. Still kicking yourself at the last one will affect the next one.

Summary

With all the distraction and the noise and the emails and phone calls, the only way to get anything done and achieve what you want to achieve is to focus on your most important, income generating tasks.

10. Not enjoying yourself

This is surely one of the most important aspects of life.

Sometimes when I [Rob] am doing some of our internet work, I forget that I should be having fun. I do all of the fun stuff like html, video coding, page architecture, email and auto-responder creation and management, data accrual and sensitivity analysis. Fun.

Sometimes my computer serves the sole purpose of pissing me off. The internet, software and technology seem to have a little Gremlins life of their own. I swear they are all laughing at me. I swear they are the voices in my head. I swear they are plotting to take over my life, abduct my girlfriend and my Dog and take me hostage.

I do occasionally have a few words with my technology to tell it who is boss. I do sometimes lose my cool and a Baron Greenback fist might hit the desk. It has been known that a phone might fly out of my office across the open plan [what did the phone do?] and I did once smash a computer [in my previous life] for messing with me.
It never did do it again though.

Sometimes, I forget that the life I have is fun and I should be enjoying the process. It is only momentary, however. Ultimately, at the end of every day I'm grateful and thankful for what I have and what we've built. I can walk away with a smile on my face knowing that I have a good life and I enjoy it.

If you don't enjoy what you're doing with your life then there's no point in doing it; it's just not worth it. It's easy to forget, and yes we all have and are allowed our off days, but if you enjoy yourself it doesn't really matter what you're doing.

Enjoy yourself, enjoy the journey; enjoy the ride. Buckle up it's going to be fast, it's going to be exciting, put the roof down and the music on full and live your life like you would if you had all the money in the world. If you enjoy yourself then people will feed off that and you'll attract people and success in abundance.

Summary

We're not here long in the grand scheme of things; life is far too short to do things we hate. How can you make money, build your portfolio and enjoy the process? What is your passion? Remember to enjoy what you do, because sometimes we all forget.

Section 7: What Are You Going to Do Now?

A quick breath: that's nearly all the information you need. Now it's time to take some action and turn your knowledge into cash [only if that is OK with you of course]...

5 The magic number

So what is the magic number? Well yes, we have told you it is 5, but what does that mean?

In our buying experience, and having met and modelled some of the most successful Property investors, we have calculated that 5 properties in your portfolio is the magic number to be able to comfortably live without the need for work.

5 properties bought in the next year at 23% below market value all valued at around £125,000 will give you instant equity of £143,750. At 8% growth as an average over the long term, you'll make over £50,000 per year compounded growth. You can view the exact figures on pages 397-8.

If you decide to take that cash tax free then you will have a net figure that is over twice the average London wage.

In a nutshell: your financial independence, your security and a passive income that you should be able to live on for the rest of your life [and beyond].

5+ is the number of properties that will allow you [picture this] holidays in the sun every year, shopping trips and relaxing spa sessions, Callaway Golf clubs and long weekends free to use them to shoot under par scores, convertible Mercedes' ski trips and Rolex watches, Chloe handbags and anything else that you could imagine that you would love to have and not have to work for.

Of course we all have different expectations of what our finances and future should look like. If you want more? Just buy more Property using the same strategy. Replicate success.

It's also possible to buy this amount of Property part time or full time. It's possible to buy this amount of Property with no money, one deposit pot or cash you can borrow from a bank. It is possible to buy this amount of Property with equity that you have in your own home, right now.

Most people will never ever have a clue how to do this. Most people will never ever believe it can be done; because most people live in the world of 'I don't know what I don't know so it can't be done.' Most people live in fear and are waiting for everyone else to do it first [social proof].

In 5 years from now those who did not take action will lose out to the *tune of over £200,000* [equity and growth of 5 properties].

See pages 397-8 for exact figures.

That's a very expensive waiting game, don't you think?!

We've all been there. I watched a development go up from £65,000 on release to nearly £200,000 in the space of 4 years and did nothing. Oh, there it goes again, another £30,000 up on last year. And still I did nothing. My Dad was telling me to buy but everyone else was telling me to wait and that I didn't know enough or have enough experience.

We use growth figures of 8% for our calculations, well below the actual current and historical average of 11.74 % since 1952. We like to be safe.

If you want to be extra cautious, use 5%. Your total portfolio would still be up at over £750,000. See page 397.

5 properties in 5 years will give you a portfolio worth **£850,306**. That will have equity of around **£226,725** [your mortgages taken from your total portfolio value]. See page 398.

Growing at 8% per year you will earn £73,466 in your first year. If you want to be extra safe then let's call it 5%: you will be earning £45,917 per year compounding [tax free].

We said that the average London wage is around £35,000 currently. If we multiply that by 2 and take off the tax and national insurance, that works at around £40,000 net earnings [less than your portfolio at a conservative 5% that will earn for you while you sleep!].

There we go. Perhaps we are making it sound too simple? We hope so, because it really is. Why pay tax? Why work in a job you hate? Why work at all if you don't want to?

We have experienced this same effect, but with a much larger portfolio and much higher growth figures. Investors who made hay in the late 90's and early 2000's would have **experienced even more growth and tax free earnings**.

Rob Moore & Mark Homer

Summary

You only need 5 investment properties to be financially secure and independent for life. You can probably access enough money from the equity in your house to build that portfolio now and release money incrementally, tax free, through remortgage. You could quite easily buy them in one good year working part time on Property in the current market.

Decide on Your strategy

Unfortunately, we know that 90% of people who read this book will now go and do nothing. Statistically the sofa, the Playstation 2, the Pub, the bingo hall and the bookies are all far more appealing than getting up, going out and making cash in a Property market crash! Now we know that is not you, but that fact still remains.

Knowing that you want to do something about it; you have 2 choices [you have dismissed the watch Big Brother and do nothing strategy, haven't you?]:

Strategy 1.

Take everything that you have learned here and go out and get your 5 properties. Then buy 5 more and 5 more and keep going as long as you desire. You really can do it. It won't always be simple, but nothing that ever meant anything was. It will take time, effort, dedication, money and hard work; but you really can do it.

You can make real cash now with big discounts with what you have learned, and then make cash through growth when the market picks up again [which it will], so *take action quickly*.

It can be done part time to start with. We know plenty of investors and people who have been on our mentorships who have bought that volume and more just doing Property on a Saturday.

Paul Webb invested in a mentorship with Mark and went on to buy 4 properties in 8 weeks from a completely standing start. You can view a video of him chatting about what he has done here:

www.progressiveproperty.co.uk/paul-webb

Once you get to that magic number it will become more serious for you. You will have seen it work and make you cash, and you may want it as a full time career, so you need to think about that [and if you want it to be that way for you].

If you follow the principles and 'secret' tips in this book, and its sister book "The 44 Most Closely Guarded property Secrets," and if you use them as a manual then you will succeed; guaranteed. So many people before you have done exactly that using exactly the same tools and tricks, and most of them started from a similar position as you, if not further back.

Rob started with £30,000 worth of debt and over £20,000 per year in interest payments on loans and credit cards. Mark started with a very basic salary and a very small amount of business knowledge.

You know you can raise finance, despite what everyone is saying at the moment, because you get what you focus on. We are still getting finance. The banks will always need to lend money one way or another.

No matter where you are in your life, and no matter what your financial position, you can get started right away by setting your strategy, rules and systems in place and make it happen.

You don't need us. You can become a full-time Property investor and you can **make whatever wealth you want to make and beyond**. Please just make sure you tell us all about your successes, we would love to know and be a part of it in some way.

Please email us with your successes and share them with us, and if you have any questions at all we will be happy to answer them and help you along your way:

robmoore@progressiveproperty.co.uk

Strategy 2.

Perhaps you don't have the time that others have to become a full time investor. Perhaps you don't have the inclination. Perhaps you want all the benefits with none of the drawbacks: you **want the baby without the labour pains**!

Perhaps you already love what you do and you just want to take the money and run? Perhaps you want to accelerate your earning time by not having to go through the experience process [because you want to earn on your portfolio in the meantime]? Perhaps you want to utilise [leverage] the knowledge and experience of the experts who are already doing it for themselves?

If this is the case then we can help you, and would love to help you. We can save you time and make you money by building and managing a **hands-free Property portfolio** that you can retire on; enjoying financial independence.

You can read the testimonials anywhere on our site where we add them all the time. After all, evidence is important:

www.progressiveproperty.co.uk/home/testimonials

We can help you if you are young or not so young. If you have savings or equity in your Property then we can build you a portfolio that at current rates will comfortably earn you well in excess of **£50,000** per year tax free [at just over 5% growth]. All you will have to do is sign papers. You can have an asset base that has cost you nothing in time but given you choice, freedom, passive income and something to pass on to your children [if you have/plan to have any].

This is the fifth and final stage of the Property investor.

Perhaps you want to do both. Perhaps you would like to earn while you are learning and you would like to learn from us. The point is you can and you have the choice now.

If you would like us to help you it couldn't be simpler. You can reach either or both of us at the following now:

Call us:
0845 1309505

Email us:
robmoore@progressiveproperty.co.uk
markhomer@progressiveproperty.co.uk

Enquire on our website:

www.progressiveproperty.co.uk

Reserve a seat at our next open day and see us speak:

www.progressiveproperty.co.uk/open-day-offer

Sign up for our free newsletter [worth £47 each]:
[You can read a years back issues for free]

www.progressiveproperty.co.uk/home/newsletter/

Buy a copy of "The 44 Most Closely Guarded Property Secrets"

www.progressiveproperty.co.uk/book-buy-now

We would love to chat to you; or even better, meet you personally.

As you know, we love people who take action. Everything in this book is about becoming informed and them **making a commitment to taking immediate and decisive action now** to create the life that you want and deserve.

Procrastination is a disease and life rewards momentum.

Because of this, because of your commitment of money and time to go through this journey with us, we have a special, limited, once only offer for you now.

Let us warn you, this is **only** for you if you are **serious** about creating **long term wealth.**

You may also need to meet out criteria to become one of our close

Rob Moore & Mark Homer

community of successful Property investors. This a mouth watering offer, that if you read the next section now, you may be able to take advantage of.

But only if you are serious now...

Are you sitting on an asset?

Over 50 % of people *don't even know* that they can do this...

How would you like to be financially independent, living your life of choice, with no loss of your time, all from the equity you have in your house, right now?

And you don't even have to sell your house or pay anything out of your own pocket or earnings.

Imagine creating your dream life from an asset that you already have now...

It is simple, easy to follow, will take you very little time and you can start right away without any knowledge of Property.

So many people who have become financially independent have accessed their money through remortgage of their existing home. Many of them have gone on to become multi-millionaires. You can do the same now.

Many people don't even realise the asset they were literally sitting on. You probably have a house that you live in. If not you will know someone who does, perhaps a friend or family member.

You may well have lived in your house for a while. Perhaps you have a small mortgage on it, perhaps you have no mortgage on it at all. You probably have equity in it, sitting idle and not being leveraged? You should be very excited now if you fit into any of these categories.

Rob Moore & Mark Homer

Perhaps you have sold a business and are looking for ways to invest for your future and you don't trust the pension system. There are many people who become divorced and are looking to consolidate and earn for the future.

The major benefit of this strategy is that your income and savings are not impacted in any way. If you have a Property with sufficient equity in it you could use the following strategy to invest without increasing your outgoings:

A typical example:

Your existing Property [home]:
Property worth £250,000
Repayment mortgage of £100,000 at £700pcm approx
£150,000 equity

Your re-mortgage:

New mortgage of £212,500 (85% of £250,000)
New interest only repayments of £1,325pcm approx
Old mortgage paid off leaving *£112,500* (less fees)

Investment Strategy:

Bank Contingency of £20,000
Invest £62,500
Bank increase in mortgage payments for 6 years: £30,000

With no change to your current circumstances you can set up your long term future for life now.

This is a typical example that someone would use when they invest with us at Progressive Property. We help you turn one Property into 6 in 6 years, and *help you earn 6 times as much per year without having to work at it*.

Imagine now what that could mean for your life. Actually take a little time to picture it...

What is it that you really want? Is it freedom and spare time to spend with friends and family? Is it the choice to follow your passion and do what you have always wanted to [that doesn't rely on you working or earning a wage]?

What things do you want that will give you a feeling of reward and satisfaction? Perhaps Cars, Watches and holidays make life more enjoyable for you. Most of us like to travel and see new things.

It has taken us over 5 years of buying Property to refine a system that can make Property investment accessible to most people. We have created a systemised 'Portfolio Building Machine,' that takes the human error out of successful Property investment

It is not for everyone; it is only for you if you are serious about creating long term wealth, but it can be for you if:

-You want it to be

-You have equity in your home that is sitting idle and not being leveraged. Perhaps you have a redundancy, you have sold a business, have a divorce settlement or have access to cash

-You want to earn a passive income of over £50,000 per year, tax free, without working or using your own time

-You want all of the benefits of Property investment, especially the cash, but do not want to spend years trying to become an expert

If you have a home that you own with a reasonable amount of equity in it, [90% of the people who are already doing it did it this way] then you should be very excited now.

Remember we talked about the relationship between money, work and stress in "The 44 Most Closely Guarded Property Secrets?" Maybe you don't want to continue working forever for 50 hours a week with little hope for future wealth and happiness in a job you don't like, with people you don't like. The government will *not* look after you and your family and your pension will probably not give you the lifestyle you want.

Maybe you imagine peace of mind and security; something that can help you enjoy the finer things in life, whatever they are to you. Perhaps even a little fun and adventure? If you don't want any of the stress but you want all of the benefits of more than enough money to retire with, then you can have it all, now.

So if you're serious about long term wealth you need to log on now:

www.progressiveproperty.co.uk/save15k

This offer of saving £15,000 will only last for a very limited time, for this particular [and small] run of this book and our open days. We like to produce small runs of the book so that we can keep updating it and improving it; and only get a few thousand printed at any one time, which usually sell very fast.

This time sensitive offer is only open to 3 people per month, we very often have a waiting list and there are 1,000's of people who are reading this book right now:

www.progressiveproperty.co.uk/save15k

For more information all you have to do is ask. Remember it is immediate action that gets results:

Call us:
0845 1309505

Email us:
robmoore@progressiveproperty.co.uk
markhomer@progressiveproperty.co.uk

Enquire on our website:
www.progressiveproperty.co.uk

Reserve a seat at our next open day:
www.progressiveproperty.co.uk/open-day-offer

Rob Moore & Mark Homer

Sign up for our free newsletter:

[You can read a years back issues for free]

www.progressiveproperty.co.uk/home/newsletter/

Buy a copy of "The 44 Most Closely Guarded Property Secrets"

www.progressiveproperty.co.uk/book-buy-now

A final note [until next time]

Well there is nothing left to say. Now you have to make your own choice. Are you going to take action on what you have read and be one of the few that succeed? Are you going to "Make Cash in a Property Market Crash?"

Just by reading this book you have proven that you want something more. Out of every thousand people who have been exposed to this book, only *you and one other* have made it this far. An amazing statistic isn't it?

And only one of the 2 of you left will go out and take action now. We sincerely hope it is you.

Please accept the biggest thank you for reading our book and being a significant part in another huge chapter in both of our lives; we look forward to speaking to you personally now.

Rob Moore & Mark Homer

About Mark & Rob

This seems like a good time to tell you a little more about us.

This book is not about us, it is about what you can do with your financial future and how you can have security and wealth through Property. However you could be asking the question:

"Who are these guys and why should I trust them?"

Just before we start, we have something very important to tell you. You will remember from our first book that Mark offered a select few mentorships at a significantly reduced price because we were filming for our latest Property DVD educational pack to be released later this year.

Mark filled the 9 places as soon as the book was released and proceeded to do just 12 mentorships. You will see the results that people have been getting on the next page [in grey text].

Even though we know that we can buy Property at ridiculous discounts, and we knew that people could copy us and do the same, we still didn't think that many people would actually go out and do it.

It's not because we didn't want them to go out and buy hugely discounted Property, or because we didn't help them [we gave away over £4,000 worth of bonuses and follow up sessions with the mentorship], it was because we understand the 80/20 principle.

We honestly thought that most people would get back into the swing of their normal life, and they would forget to take action.

We have been amazed with the results. They have completely surprised us because we have only mentored 12 people and we are smashing the statistics.

Because of this, Mark has finally given in to my nagging, and will run more mentorships. His time is worth £517 per hour, so the value you get having him for a whole day is substantial.

He also gets benefit, because he gets to learn about other cities across the UK [he comes to your home town or 'patch'] and his knowledge has grown to be breathtaking [he's teaching me all sorts at the moment about the South, Wigan, Hull, Leeds, Brighton, Lincoln, Corby and most parts of London].

There is a catch to this. He can only do 3 per month because it takes one day of research and one day on the mentorship, and that's all the time we can afford to have him out of our businesses. And he's been fully booked from March to the middle of July.

Of course, we've talked about social proof and you're going to want to see evidence of these results, so please visit this page now:

www.progressiveproperty.co.uk/mentorships

We want committed and serious people who will follow the strategies that Mark teaches and take action on what he says, because *we know that people will make money doing just that*.

Benchmarking, scraping and taking *proven blueprints that make cash*.

We have also created some *Fast Action* bonuses worth over £2,000 to give you a compelling reason to take action now.

If you would feel that what you have read in this book is of value and you would like to be personally shown by Mark how to buy Property at 30% below market value [over and over], then this might be for you. If you log on now and find that the offer has expired, you were just a little too late and Mark has been booked out. If you hurry now you can save over 66% by logging on to the special link below as a reader of this book

www.progressiveproperty.co.uk/mentorships

OK. We absolutely regard ourselves as 2 normal guys. We are not 'Guru's' or self proclaimed cult leaders or evangelists. We don't have a long CV of master degrees and diplomas as there are no such qualifications in the Property 'industry.' Even if there were, they would probably mean very little to us, because we like to be able to give *real life evidence and experience.*

We both started from relatively humble beginnings and are by no means self professed Property squillionaires. We do have a relatively substantial Property portfolio that we have built in a relatively short space of time, and we do have the evidence to back up our claims, and yes we have also *helped many other people do the same.*

www.progressiveproperty.co.uk/testimonials

We have 8 years combined experience in Property [and we don't mean living in our Mum's house]. We've spent nearly £700,000 accruing all of this Property knowledge and nearly 6,000 hours of our own time. Well worth your small investment so far, we believe.

We have learned what works and what does not through actual experience. We believe that we are humbly successful.

What is also so important is that we have a true passion for investing. Just the talk of investing money, finding deals with the potential to yield greater returns, and building an asset base that can fund a fast and exciting lifestyle, turns us both on big time!

Sad, isn't it? Well actually, we don't think so. Some people like fast Cars. Some people like fast women. Some people like both. Some people like shopping.

We love deals [and fast Cars and women!]. We love the fun and the challenge [and sometimes the reward of beating the odds]. We built Progressive Property around this. The contentment and value in being able to **help you do the same** is also a huge driver for us.

We started Progressive Property on £300 each and we are proud of what we have been able to achieve for ourselves and our close community of investors, in a relatively short space of time.

Mark about Mark

I had dreams of becoming an investment banker because it seemed like they earned the most money, had the most glamorous lifestyle and the most *fun*.

I soon realised that the competition was intense and I would not even be considered with my grades [although I enjoyed university very much]. I hit a wall because I had been working to this point for many years of my life.

I made money in the interim in true entrepreneurial fashion selling various products; importing and exporting, and raised enough capital to be able to start investing.

Following University I went on to work for a multinational company on a graduate scheme. I thought I would be an integral part of a big company with great prospects.

As it turns out I was a glorified butcher earning average money with little future. I didn't like the corporate 'way' and the hierarchy. Looking up at someone's ass on a ladder I was at the bottom of was not my idea of happiness and freedom; having to wait in line for mediocre 'success' and 'status.'

I looked at the guys 20 years ahead of me and I didn't like what I saw. They were wrinkled, tired, financially stretched and they never looked happy. I thought to myself; all that work [weekends as well], and this is where I will be heading in 20 years?
Who wants to be like that?

Not me. No Thank You! I wasn't that happy. My zest, enjoyment and passion had been sapped.

I joined a Property investment company thinking that I could change my life by becoming a business owner. I was made a director for impressive Property sales however the reality was that I was a glorified employee. My boss certainly didn't look happy or live the kind of life which I aspired to, even though he 'read all of the books' and 'did not deal with negativity.' I didn't want to model him.

I was genuinely down at this point; nothing seemed to be going right. I wasn't sleeping for months on end because of the worry of work, and it began to affect my personal and working life.

Yeah on the outside I had the job title, yeah I was investing, and yes I was making money. But I wasn't happy.

And that is what is most important for me. For all of us, I think.
Then I met Rob. He joined the company I was at and we hit it off immediately. He was [and still is] a qualified life coach.

We struck up a gentleman's deal that he would coach me in areas like relationships, health/body, work, spirituality and I would teach him how to invest and make money.

This is where my whole life changed. We got on so well and our skills seemed to dovetail. Whatever Rob was weak at I could help him with and vice versa.

Over a period of months I learned how to develop every area of my life to become the best that I could be. I started to run faster and longer than I had ever before [I now go almost everyday and for 2 months I ran every single day]. I ran a half marathon after 4 months of training and have lost a lot of weight to become fit and healthy.

Even the girls started to notice me more [I think]! I became so much better at building relationships with people and I started to feel great and love every day of my life. Now I sleep like a baby and have massive energy all day long [as long as I have been for my run and had my Supreme greens].

And you know the best bit? My Property investment ability rocketed!

We bought around 20 properties in 2006 with a relatively small amount of money and refined a Property buying system so much that we now get 15-30% discounts on *existing* [not new build] Property deals all day long. Then the articles in the major newspapers came [The Independent, The Wall Street Journal], and the TV shows [Channel 4], and it all went very wild and exciting for me in a very short space of time.

I am now happier than I have ever been in my life. Don't get me wrong, I am not a happy clappy faux positive personal development junkie. I have my moments, but I know that I am in control of my feelings, my decisions, my actions and my future, which has been a huge development in my life, and something I never truly understood before.

I am lucky [Rob does not believe in luck but I think we have had our fair share] to be where I am and have the ability and knowledge to help you do the same.

Rob about Mark

Mark is a dealmaker. He loves being on the phone and juggling many tasks at once. He has a sixth sense for Property investment deals in my opinion, and is definitely one of the most [if not *the* most] knowledgeable investors both here in Peterborough, and who I have met anywhere.

He bought some quite amazing deals in 2004/2005 when he was relatively new to the market and it was clear to me that *I had to learn what he knew*. He had a talent and was only going to get better. I wanted in on those kinds of deals.

He has helped me immensely with my Property knowledge and just being around him helps me grow immeasurably every single day.

His attention to detail is scary. To be honest sometimes he bores the pants off me with the amount of detail he goes into, but it's all good. I am one of these kinds of people who *likes the baby and not the labour pains*. I like to leverage and maximise my own time by positioning myself with people who are better than me in specialised areas. Mark actually enjoys the labour pains I think! That is one of the reasons why he is so good at what he does.

Mark continues to build our portfolio buying some ridiculously cheap Property and he gets better and better at it. I will be eternally grateful to him for that, along with a whole host of other fantastic [if slightly obsessive] traits that make him a true investor entrepreneur.

Rob about Rob

Ever since I was 17 my life seemed to go steadily downhill.

I was a talented sportsman and blitzed A's at my GCSE's [through hard work and the fear of failure, rather than talent]. I was accepted to one of the best Universities in the country and felt I had a good future ahead of me [or so I thought]...

Then in 1996 I had 2 serious injuries within the space of 6 months. I crashed my motorbike [and not by half]. It was my pride and joy at the time because I no longer looked the pillock that I did on the Moped I had previously. It took me one year of begging to let my parents to get me one. I spent 6 months in rehabilitation from multiple breaks. [If you are considering getting a motorbike: DON'T! Just don't].

That ruined any prospect of me becoming a professional Golfer or Cricketer, which I had genuine aspirations for. I held much resentment and never really recovered from that. 6 months later my appendix burst [a close run in with the big man upstairs] whilst in a nightclub. The whole second year of my A-Levels was written off.

I spent the next 7 years always living in the shadow of myself and what I could have become, but felt had been taken away from me. I lost my ability to dream and believe in myself, which sucked to be honest.

I managed to scrape into a University and pulled off a good degree in Architecture without doing any work. As soon as I graduated all I wanted to do was anything else other than Architecture. The only reason I didn't quit the course after 2 months was my pride [ego] as I did not want anyone to think that I gave up on things.

Ironically this was to serve me very well for the future.

I came back to Peterborough to help my family in their pub as my Dad was very ill. What was essentially a 3 month plan ended up being nearly 3 years. All the while I knew that this was not what I ultimately wanted to do, but it is hard to break away when you think you are letting your family down. I'm sure you may have felt the same. I finally broke away in 2003 and set out to make a living in my real true passion: Art.

I have loved Art since before I could talk and that is something that I did actually have some kind of talent for. I believed that talent was enough to bring me the success, wealth and happiness that I desired.

As it turns out talent was not enough and I began to feel dragged down. I struggled for 2 years working 16 hours a day and failing to pay my debts of over £30,000 that I amassed at [and since] university.

I felt pretty low at this point. It was impacting other areas of my life such as my relationships with friends and family and my ability to socialise and enjoy life. I had completely lost my drive and enthusiasm.

I was constantly looking back at what I should have been and that, 7 years on, I had still achieved nothing in my life that I wanted.

I realised that I had no savings, no future, and that if something happened to me I would be in big trouble. I was not looking forward to working 16 hours a day for the rest of my life. I mean, who wants that?

My Dad worked for 15 years in the RAF serving his country to receive a pension of £19 per week. £19 per week. What an absolute joke. I did not want the same fate.

That has become a huge motivator for me to succeed financially so that I can help my family and ensure the same thing does not happen to me, my girlfriend, my sister, my close friends, and people just like you.

I knew that I was missing something and in 2005 I met Mark, my business partner, great friend and investment partner. And co-author of this book, of course.

Those 2 months were the best, most exciting turning points in my life. Since then, since finding what I consider to be my purpose and true path, everything has accelerated so fast and I have learned so much that sometimes I wonder what on earth I was doing for 25 years.

Mark and I really have had the most amazing journey and I feel very fortunate [not lucky] to have forged such a relationship with such a great guy, and someone with such vast knowledge.

I was out of debt by April and in the same year [my interest payments alone were over £2,000 per month - more than I was earning!]. I reached a £1million Property portfolio in 6 months [most of which was gained through one simple remortgage of my existing house], trained as a life coach, did TV shows for Living and The Business Channel, and became MD of a Property investment company. Since then I have spoken at the biggest Property events in the country in front of hundreds of people, and I'm fortunate [not lucky] because that is something I always wanted to do.

I really don't consider this to be 'impressive.' I have a healthy caution towards 'life coaching' and Property investment, because many people are not **diligent** enough to be able to do it properly. However we're all just trying to make a living and with the right amount of application both are seriously rewarding for very different reasons.

I feel that is an area where I have vastly improved over the last few years, because my biggest problem was getting quite good at things but not **taking it that extra step**. I learned that it was the experts; the best of the best, who make all of the money.

I honestly feel that the reason I have achieved more in the last 4 years than the previous 25 and a half is not because I am anything special, but because I am doing what I truly believe in and what I have a real passion for.

If only I had started sooner, but then I guess we all say that, don't we? And I now know that *now* is always the best time.

It's funny because so many people think they have missed the boat with Property. I thought that myself for about 4 years. I was looking at 3 bed houses for £70,000 in 2003. And I did nothing [but watch them go up and up and up and tell people stories about why I didn't couldn't wouldn't shouldn't buy them]. These are worth over £200,000 now. I am just so glad that I know what I know now. **Now is always the best time**.

Things just keep moving for Mark and I now and we have newer, bigger goals. I am speaking at some of the biggest events in the UK and we continue to build our portfolio both for us and our investors daily.

The discounts Simon has been getting buying Property for us full time amaze us more and more; and that's the exciting, whirlwind of a market we are in at the moment.

We've more than 10 offers to do other TV shows, endless joint ventures and business partner alliances, and met some really great people. It is amazing what a bit of momentum can do. It is the security that I feel from having a Property portfolio that will look after me for the rest of my life that enables me to really go for it in other areas too.

And the doors to other exciting worlds that open up for you now.

Mark about Rob

It's Rob's drive and focus that inspire me the most. When I first met him he knew only the basics about Property, but within his first 9 months his portfolio was up over £1 million [and he was £30,000 in debt at the time].

I have not met many people who have the ability to do this, and the fact that he has done it in a very short space of time gives me the evidence I need to know that you can do the same.

I think it is his ability to just go for it and make things work regardless of what people say that keeps us going when many people have been saying [through the last 5 years] that the Property market is dead. If we believed them we would still be employed, and not have **the freedom we desire**; which is so important.

He learns very quickly and has seriously added to his skills since I have known him. Sometimes he thinks so much to the future that he forgets about detail, and I have had to help him with his driving licence, a couple of parking tickets, the odd speeding fine and some household insurance.

I'm not his Mum or his P.A, but we all have to make sacrifices I guess! I do have to keep him in check, but that is what having a business partner is for.

Your figures & projections

Why now is the best time to buy [for 11 years?]: Page 106

On Page 106 we were discussing what could happen for you if you just bought 5 properties through the crash.

If you just bought 5 properties this year at 30% below market value, all at around £100,000, here would be your results:

Investment Property 1: £100,000   Equity: £30,000
Investment Property 2: £100,000   Equity: £30,000
Investment Property 3: £100,000   Equity: £30,000
Investment Property 4: £100,000   Equity: £30,000
Investment Property 5: £100,000   Equity: £30,000

Total Equity: £150,000

Side note: it is unlikely that you would buy all 5 properties at exactly £100,000. If you bought them all within a one year period, they would all be around that figure, as an average.

Investment Property 1: £100,000   Cashflow: £600 p/a
Investment Property 2: £100,000   Cashflow: £600 p/a
Investment Property 3: £100,000   Cashflow: £600 p/a
Investment Property 4: £100,000   Cashflow: £600 p/a
Investment Property 5: £100,000   Cashflow: £600 p/a

Cashflow figures are taken at £50 pcm [net]. Loan to value can affect cashflow figures.

Rob Moore & Mark Homer

Average growth on each Property [at 5%]:

Year 1: value: £100,000:   growth: £5,000
Year 2: value £105,000:   growth: £5,250
Year 3: value: £110,250:   growth: £5,513
Year 4: value £115,763:   growth: £5,788
Year 5: value £121,551:   growth: £6,078

Total growth per Property: £21,551

Average growth over the portfolio [5 properties]:

Year 1: value: £500,000:   growth: £25,000
Year 2: value £525,000:   growth: £26,250
Year 3: value: £551,250:   growth: £27,563
Year 4: value £578,813:   growth: £28,941
Year 5: value £607,754:   growth: £30,388

Total growth over the 5 properties: £107,754

Side note: we have used 5% growth over the next 5 years, less than half of the average growth, because of the current market. You should do your figures conservatively in this market, and no one really knows when growth will return.

Rental growth at £50 pcm per year [£600 per year: roughly 5%] per Property:

Year 1: value: £100,000:   cashflow: £600 p/a
Year 2: value £105,000:   cashflow: £1,200 p/a
Year 3: value: £110,250:   cashflow: £1,800 p/a
Year 4: value £115,763:   cashflow: £2,400 p/a
Year 5: value £121,551:   cashflow: £3,000 p/a

Cashflow from each Property in 5 years: £3,000 [net]

Rental growth over the 5 properties:

Year 1: value: £500,000:   cashflow: £3,000 p/a
Year 2: value £525,000:   cashflow: £6,000 p/a
Year 3: value: £551,250:   cashflow: £9,000 p/a
Year 4: value £578,813:   cashflow: £12,000 p/a
Year 5: value £607,754:   cashflow: £15,000 p/a

Cashflow from each Property in 5 years: £15,000 [net]

Motivated seller script: Page 165

Here is the script that you will find very useful for pre-qualifying motivated sellers:

First name:
Last name:
Home phone No:
Mobile phone no:
Email address:
The best time to contact you:
What is your Property address [inc. Postcode]:

Why are you selling?

What type of Property is it?
Are you living there are the moment?
Estimated value:
Current mortgage outstanding:
How quickly would you like to sell?
What is most important to you in selling your Property?

Do you have any other loans or charges secured on your Property?

Would you like to sell and rent back?
Where did you hear about us?

Stage 4: the leveraged investor: Page 253 & 254

A Property has been bought for £100,000 but it's actually worth £135,000. You get an initial mortgage of 20% of £100,000 and then you remortgage to 80% of £135,000, therefore you can get your deposit back out. Here is an example below assuming no refurbishment work is needed:

Purchase price: £100,000
Market value [reval]: £135,000
Rent: £595

First mortgage [80% inc. Fee]: £80,497
Deposit: £20,000
Legal costs for purchase: £1,000
Purchase valuation: £300
Legal costs for remortgage: £750
Remortgage valuation: £300
Cashflow requirement: £2,000
Total money to acquire: £24,350

Revaluation: £135,000
New mortgage: £108,000
Minus purchase mortgage: £80,497
Minus lenders closing fees: £350

Leaves balance of: £27,153
Minus total to acquire: £24,350
Cash surplus: £2,803

Rules: Page 262

Example cashflow analysis of a Property per month [pcm]:

Monthly rent: £595

Management: £74.38 [12.5%]
Gas safety testing: £6.67 [£80 per year]
Maintenance: £12.50 [£150 per year]
Voids: £22.82 [2 weeks per year]
Bad debt: £11.41 [1 week per year]

Total: £128.23 pcm

You may have to include service charge and ground rent for flats

Your values: Page 312

What are the things that are most important to you in your life? The things that excite you, drive you and make you jump out of bed in the morning? Ask yourself the following very important question:

'What is the most important thing for me in the area of Property and business?'

1.
2.
3.
4.
5.
6.
7.
8.
9.
10.

Limit your list to 10, any others will probably not be high enough to really drive you or be important. If you hit some 'blank spots,' where you are struggling to fill the 10 spaces, then don't worry. Push through it, you'll get there. Perhaps take a little break or clear your mind.

Your findings should be very interesting. If particular traits that you feel are important [perhaps making money, fun or focus] aren't as high on the list as perhaps you feel they need to be to succeed, look at re-ordering your values to get the results that you really want, not what you are comfortable with. Try changing the order now:

1.
2.
3.
4.
5.
6.
7.
8.
9.
10.

Have fun with this process, it can be very powerful. You can also do it for other areas of your life such as health and relationships.

5 The magic number: Page 355/6

5 Property portfolio growth at 8% per year:

Property 1 in 1st year: value £125,000. Value in year 5: £170,061
Property 2 in 2nd year: value £135,000. Value in year 5: £170,061
Property 3 in 3rd year: value £145,800. Value in year 5: £170,061
Property 4 in 4th year: value £157,464. Value in year 5: £170,061
Property 5 in 5th year: value £170,061. Value in year 5: £170,061

Total value: *£850,306*

5 Property portfolio growth at 5% per year:

Property 1 in 1st year: value £125,000. Value in year 5: £151,938
Property 2 in 2nd year: value £131,250. Value in year 5: £151,938
Property 3 in 3rd year: value £137,813. Value in year 5: £151,938
Property 4 in 4th year: value £144,703. Value in year 5: £151,938
Property 5 in 5th year: value £151,938. Value in year 5: £151,938

Total value: *£759,691*

5 Property portfolio at historical growth of 11.74% per year:

Property 1 in 1st year: value £125,000. Value in year 5: £194,869
Property 2 in 2nd year: value £139,675. Value in year 5: £194,869
Property 3 in 3rd year: value £156,073. Value in year 5: £194,869
Property 4 in 4th year: value £174,396. Value in year 5: £194,869
Property 5 in 5th year: value £194,869. Value in year 5: £194,869

Total value: *£974,349*

Equity in your portfolio at 8% growth:

[Total value of Property minus initial 85% mortgage]:

Property 1 in 1st year: value £170,061.   Equity: £63,811

Property 2 in 2nd year: value £170,061.   Equity: £55,311

Property 3 in 3rd year: value £170,061.   Equity: £46,131

Property 4 in 4th year: value £170,061.   Equity: £36,217

Property 5 in 5th year: value £170,061.   Equity: £25,509

Total equity from valuation: **£226,979**

You could nearly double that equity buying at 30% BMV in the market now.

To buy a copy of our first book and companion to this, "The 44 Most Closely Guarded Property Secrets" please visit:

www.progressiveproperty.co.uk/book-buy-now

Remember that you can be, do and have anything you want. Never let the Sheep or Crabs tell you otherwise. Take care now...

Rob Moore & Mark Homer